ACCLAIM

"Great leadership is about what you see for a living - not just what you do for a living and "Zoom Leadership" is all about the wisdom of seeing clearly."
Michael Carroll, author of *The Mindful Leader*

"Based on a disarmingly simple theoretical model: Think- Act-Feel-Witness, the added value of Janet Britcher's book Zoom Leadership lies in the many concrete examples she provides from her experience as a coach, mentor and trainer in the business world. These concepts and examples are a timely reminder that leadership roles and responsibilities are shared not only between colleagues, but also with the trainer herself, and that all parties may then grow through the process."
Michael Luke, Regional Training Manager, World Rugby and Adjunct Professor, Boston University

"Filled with straightforward, clear guidance Britcher's Zoom Leadership is dead on. It's filled with practical, grounded advice on leading effectively in today's challenging work environments, Zoom Leadership accelerates learning for leaders and their team members. Britcher shows how changing focus to create new insights insures a healthier, more effective workplace."
Alesia Latson, President, Latson Leadership Group, author of *More Time For You: A Powerful System to Organize Your Work and Get Things Done*

"Four letters for this book, one word – ZOOM! It's an essential roadmap for leaders to zero in on what they need to do, and focus on the highest-gain activities. No matter where you are on your leadership journey, you can learn something from this book – guaranteed."
Beverly Flaxington, author, *Understanding Other People: The Five Secrets to Human Behavior* and *Make Your Shift: The Five Most Powerful Moves You Can Make to Get Where You Want to Go*

ZOOM LEADERSHIP

CHANGE YOUR FOCUS, CHANGE YOUR INSIGHTS

JANET L. BRITCHER

Publisher's Information

Published by Leadership Alchemy Press

ISBN 978-0-9988006-0-8

Book design and distribution, Ebook Bakery

Cover design, Leslie McGrath,
mcgrathillustration.com

Author contact: janet@transformationmanagement.com

© 2017 by Janet L Britcher

ALL RIGHTS RESERVED

Author's Note: All of the conversations transcribed in this book occurred with leaders, but their names and identifying details have been changed to protect confidentiality.

For information contact: P.O. Box 320552, Boston, MA 02132. Printed in the United States of America.

Acknowledgments

I am grateful to the hundreds of clients who have participated in leadership workshops and coaching sessions. I am grateful they shared their challenges, concerns, insights, joys, sorrows, and triumphs, and for the opportunity to support them and provide perspective.

I also want to thank:

Kurt Leland, my first reader, who provided immediate encouragement, and for his suggestions about the book's structure. I am also grateful for the many years he has been my intuition teacher.

Steve Davis, for encouragement and enthusiasm, who was ready to pre-order as soon he read the introduction.

Ray Welbaum who instantly understood the value of changing perspective, and provided helpful edits.

Jen Guilleman, for her open heart, passion for leadership, and for providing early feedback and edits to improve clarity.

For my community of colleagues who nurture, support and encourage me in so many ways: Perry Carrison, Beverly Flaxington, Alesia Latson, Sophie Parker, Trish Perry, Bob Ross, John Roberts, Beth Shapiro, and Wynne Miller.

To my parents, Mary and Bill Britcher, who fostered love of words throughout my life, and from whom I inherited this humble and empowering view of learning: "I don't know but I can find out."

DEDICATION

To my clients, in gratitude for all we learn together

CONTENTS

Introduction...xi

Chapter 1: Zoom Leadership: A New View 1

Chapter 2: Lens One—Think 29

Chapter 3: Lens Two—Act... 69

Chapter 4: Lens Three—Feel 99

Chapter 5: Lens Four—Witness....................................143

Chapter 6: Zoom Leadership at the Movies.......................173

Chapter 7: Applying the Model..................................181

Epilogue 191

Sources 194

Workshops..196

About the Author...197

INTRODUCTION

To change ourselves effectively, we first had to change our perceptions.
—Stephen R. Covey

Every day, my leadership clients challenge themselves to raise the bar of their performance and improve their skill sets and competencies. As a result, their organizations are growing and transforming around them. Their attention is naturally focused on their organization and staff, the requirements of their role, their functional expertise (marketing, operations, engineering, and so on), and their future strategy. My responsibility as a coach is to understand their languages and worlds so I may provide them with practical, handy tools that help them view their businesses from fresh perspectives. With this book I offer some of my techniques which have been effective and transformational for my clients.

Most of us have made our worlds smaller than they need to be. I hope to open up worlds by sharing the Zoom Leadership model with you. I invite you to adapt and modify it, apply it with other familiar models, and synthesize and update it to your needs like an enduring folk song that morphs over time. It is not intended to be a complete leadership approach, nor is it designed to oversimplify the mysterious forces—conscious and unconscious—that drive us, confuse us, or contradict our own stated goals or values.

What Is *Zoom Leadership*?

Zoom Leadership can be a simple, yet powerful approach for leaders when implemented properly. I define it in the following manner:

> *Zoom Leadership is a streamlined approach to exploring and altering perspective to create insightful options when faced with seemingly intractable problems.*

Over the years I have come across many instances of business professionals who struggled a great deal with their dilemmas. One such individual, Rachel, found herself constantly under siege. She had been with the company nine years, a lot longer than many of her counterparts. As a result, she had vast knowledge about the company, its history, and processes. She felt strong devotion and loyalty to the company, as well as a strong sense of teamwork, and ended up taking on tasks that were significantly outside the scope of her role in order to assist people in other departments. Often she worked at the office late into the evening.

Rachel objected to how others in her organization tended to have an individual focus, unaware of the impact of their words. Coworkers would sometimes be careless about how they represented the company in client meetings. Some blatantly criticized the company to a client. Others apologized for a delay in responsiveness when the client was actually at fault.

That wasn't all. Rachel was frustrated that people from other departments repeatedly asked her for the same information. Rachel felt that the supervisors and managers of their respective departments should serve as more responsible resources for their team members.

On the one hand, Rachel felt she had a big picture perspective: She was at looking at the interests of the company as a whole. She was invested in its long-term success—professionally and personally. She wanted to be helpful, so she kept adding more to her already filled plate.

On the other hand, she felt her company's implementation team had a responsibility to offer better training, improve access to knowledge, establish quality control measures, improve their processes, and create and analyze metrics (such as weekly reporting) that would reveal issues before they were stumbled upon.

Rachel had already "zoomed out" to *Thinking* about the big picture. She had also simultaneously "zoomed in" to notice errors in details. However, the Action she had "zoomed in" on involved her taking on too much work. Her reluctance to push back on her workload was due to Feelings of commitment and responsibility to the company and the clients. Eventually, I envisioned Rachel heading towards burnout.

I was well aware of the company's growth plans and thought that Rachel's heroic measures were never going to be enough. I posed the following question to her: "What do you think would happen if you were to focus all of your thoughts and energy on sustainability and scalability?" She carefully considered that reframe. Suddenly, her perspective "zoomed out." She realized that taking on workload and problems from her colleagues was only enabling what she perceived as their laziness. Contrary to her intentions, her rescue efforts were holding them back from learning opportunities. Once she drew this conclusion, she felt liberated about saying "No" to people when they were looking for her fix their problems for them or take up their slack. She resolved to try this new approach, although moving out of her habitual helpfulness would be challenging. She could see the payoff for the company. Zooming out to place sustainability and scalability in her field of vision enabled her to Think and Feel differently, which meant she could *Act differently*.

Zoom In and Zoom Out

My experience from over twenty years of executive and organizational coaching has shown me that *changing one's perspective* is the single most important strategy leaders can use—not only when confronting a seemingly insurmountable challenge, but also when creating a vision and leading the team on a daily basis.

My work is informed by diverse study of human behavior and psychology, the exciting, emerging fields of neurology and leadership, and the kinesthetic somatic (body) awareness and leadership. Zoom Leadership integrates my understanding and appreciation of businesses and how they accomplish the following:

- Organize departments and workflow
- Distribute authority
- Accomplish goals

- Create culture
- Develop staff
- Engage ideas

In the chapters that follow I offer an approach that simplifies and accelerates leadership impact when running meetings, planning, strategizing, managing, and delegating. My intent is that you will discover fresh perspectives, incorporate new behaviors, and develop increased self-confidence.

Attention—Where Is Your Focus?

Before our current digital era, access to knowledge and information was a scarce resource and a key to power and impact. Centuries ago, books were only available in private collections. Education was private—for the elite and wealthy—and restricted by class and gender. Today, however, we are in a wonderful age of information. We have far more information than we can handle, with access to all of it right at our fingertips. We can pursue whatever topics or facts prompt our curiosity any time of day, as long as we have power cords, outlets (or chargers), and Internet access.

Our scarce resource is *attention span* and being able to stay focused and get things done without the distraction of so much accessible data. A critical aspect of being a great leader is being able to devote enough attention to a problem in order to solve it or create something new.

In order to reclaim your attention—which you may not even realize has dissipated—you must learn how to quickly *reframe*: to look at a familiar situation from a fresh, more empowering and effective point of view. Reframing leads to several positive outcomes:

- Improved relationship skills—working well with diverse people
- Greater self-awareness—noticing reactions at the intellectual, emotional, and physical levels

- Deeper understanding of values—knowing the foundation that provides confidence and clarity
- Clearer life purpose—awareness of the daily contributions and lasting legacy that motivate oneself and others

With regard to the final point above, leaders who are aligned with their values and life purpose have more energy, vitality, results, and impact. Although the focus of my coaching is leadership, clients frequently tell me that the new perspectives they gained from this approach have benefited them in other areas of their lives:

- Peace of mind about nagging problems
- Work/life balance
- Family dynamics
- Community activities, such as volunteering

Keeping It Straightforward

Although an appreciation for complexity can provide insight, my preference is to offer tools and techniques that distill complexity into simple, easy terms. When I work with clients I feel a responsibility not to speak in jargon; I offer them ordinary, succinct words and experiences that open their worlds—so they may open themselves to their own vast possibilities. While I love complex theories and concepts of human behavior, psychology, and emotion, I also recognize that we live in a world where learning happens in ordinary, messy, everyday interactions. These interactions can be glossed over or explored and expanded, depending on our habits of mind.

By encouraging leaders to "move in and out" to view their perceptions of reality, Zoom Leadership provides an immediate visceral experience, an altering of the status quo. It can be illuminating or disturbing as our sense of the world as we know it becomes reordered. It provides quick access to options, yet it also can be profound in terms of gained insights.

Most of us habitually use the zoom feature on a cellphone camera or video camera to alter the size and scope of the subject. Online maps and apps also allow us to quickly change the size and scope of the area. Leaders I've worked with have found *zooming* to be a comfortable, yet provocative metaphor to consider new options.

Leaders are best served when they can remain grounded in their current knowledge of how things get done while at the same time altering their perspectives. After all, as a leader you know your world better than anyone else does; I would never tell a client how to conduct his or her business. My goal is to maintain and improve upon what works by helping you see things differently and more clearly.

How This Book Is Organized

Chapter One outlines the Zoom Leadership model and provides brief examples.

Chapters Two through Five apply the Zoom Leadership model through each of the four lenses of human experience:

- *Think*: This is the most common lens in business: problem solving, analysis, strategy, planning, and reasoning. It is often the most comfortable lens for leaders to discuss and focus on.
- *Act*: This is the next most common lens, because businesses must take Action in order to create products or provide services for their clients. Businesses are a hive of activities, and many leaders spend their time in this mode. This is the lens through which experimentation and productivity occur.
- *Feel*: This lens has received increasing respect over the last decade or so. Greater emphasis has been placed on the long-term relationship value of empathy and emotional intelligence. This direction has been bolstered by brain scans revealing what happens during decision-making. (Hint: It's not the logical part of the brain that is activated.)
- *Witness*: This last lens is a word we don't hear a lot in business, and therefore I'm going to advocate for

it. Witness is a form of mindfulness and reflection. It's a way of being truly present and conveying this to others.

Chapter Six applies zooming to movies. Movies are one way of storytelling: of listening for the essence of the human condition. In this case, the human condition of noticing how perspective is used, and how, when it changes, it changes reactions and experiences. Write-ups from these examples apply the Zoom Leadership model, as a way to deepen understanding of the approach. Movie producers never knew what a rich experience they would offer us for this technique!

Chapter Seven provides an opportunity to practice the Zoom Leadership approach.

Now that you know a little about me and have a basic understanding about what I mean by Zoom Leadership, we can start to review the approach in detail in Chapter One.

1

ZOOM LEADERSHIP: A NEW VIEW

To raise new questions, new possibilities, to regard old problems from a new angle, requires creative imagination and marks real advance in science [and leadership].
—**Albert Einstein**

The power of perspective offers the potential for profound leadership insights. Altering a *view* of the facts and context opens up new ways to perceive the issue to be addressed, and therefore the available options. This flexibility of Thinking increases innovation for leadership decisions. For leaders working with a team, flexible Thinking enhances creative problem solving as well as relationships by being flexible about *how* results are achieved. This invites greater participation and ownership.

To illustrate the power of perspective, let's take the issue of missed revenue targets. Some leaders examine that by way of Thinking about the details, zooming in to see the results by product line, by month, or by sales person. Others may zoom out, comparing results for a whole year to a prior year. Others may zoom even further out, looking at percent of the market compared to competitors, or the market opportunity for a new product line. Leaders tend to replicate their own Thinking approach over time.

In responding to missed revenue targets, another leader may react first through an emotional lens, experiencing anger, frustration, or disappointment. His or her next move may be to try to motivate sales people through criticism, threats, or inspiration, appealing to their emotional response. That leader may tend to use that default approach to the exclusion of others.

Another with a bias towards action may get close to the issue by joining sales people in the field, or take action by taking a longer view and revisiting the hiring criteria or by on-boarding and training new sales people. That bias for action may be his or her usual approach.

Asking the question "What other perspective can be used here" enables leaders to enrich their problem solving by considering perspectives outside of their usual habit of Thinking. The rate of change in business is such that relying on a tried-and-true approach should be only one of several options leaders consider, in order to optimize decision-making.

On the NASA web site, you can find the following quote:

> From the dawn of humankind to a mere 400 years ago, all that we knew about our universe came through observations with the naked eye. Then Galileo turned his telescope toward the heavens in 1610. The world was in for an awakening.
> Saturn, we learned, had rings. Jupiter had moons. That nebulous patch across the center of the sky called the Milky Way was not a cloud but a collection of countless stars. Within but a few years, our notion of the natural world would be forever changed. A scientific and societal revolution quickly ensued.

You can see from the above that advancements in science and scientology resulted from the ability to zoom in. The same can happen for leaders with how they view the universe of their work environment from their leadership vantage point.

As you assess leadership decisions in your organization, envision that you have a camera or a video camera that can zoom so far out you can see a critical business issue from a view way up in the clouds to create a distanced perspective. Then, once you've captured that image, you're able to zoom in so close it's as if you can inspect the problem under a powerful microscope. In this chapter I will provide you with an introduction to all of the tools you'll need to get started in order to zoom in or out as needed.

Leaders' Zoom Technique

The leaders I work with are established and successful, but readily admit that they are still learning as their responsibilities and careers expand. One of the ways I strive to help them accelerate this growth is to encourage them to reflect on what is happening in their own individual processes. I might ask them things like "How is this similar or different from experiences in the past?" I challenge them to scrutinize which patterns of Thinking, Acting, or Feeling might be limiting their options.

Like most professionals, my clients often must balance their leadership roles with handling day-to-day functional tasks in their departmental areas (Finance, Operations, Engineering, etc.). Rapid technological advancements and other major changes (such as competition, regulatory requirements, talent availability, etc.) force them to adapt to new situations and crises while at the same time providing leadership and inspiration to their teams. Persistent, nagging challenges—or those in uncharted territory—can either generate fear (constriction) or spark renewed energy (expansion).

My coaching involves working with leaders to expand their options, open up opportunities and possibilities, and help them consider the best course for themselves in whatever situation they may be facing (such as licensing a new product, hiring a new executive, or closing a division). They are in charge of making their own choices and may already aligned with their company's principles, their job responsibilities, and their core values. It is my role to pull back the curtain a little more each time on the options without providing answers for them, which they must discover for themselves. I am there to help ensure that they don't fall back on the habits that may have worked in the past but may not have relevance to a given situation (such as handling remote teams versus co-located work situations in the past).

I have deep respect for the great variety and styles of Thinking, and I believe there are many ways to be a good leader. Some are methodical, for example, whereas others are spontaneous and innovative. I don't try to impose a new leadership style. Though there are things to be learned from other great leaders (such as Steve Jobs or Jeff Bezos), I believe my clients discover their greatest power if they are aligned (*Act*) with their own values (*Think, Feel*) and sense of purpose (*Witness*). Strength comes from self-knowledge and alignment.

I have developed the zoom technique over the years. This includes the lenses of Think, Act, Feel, and Witness, as well as "shining the light," to ensure the focus is on the right issue—and I'm delighted to share it with you. My intent is for the technique to be accessible and have the capability of being applied right away, as well as for deepening perceptions to develop solutions over the long term.

Leaders grappling with a challenge tend to express what is on their minds with energy, frustration, or enthusiasm, though not necessarily with a clear understanding or insight as to the deeper cause or next steps. For example, recently Leah was complaining about one of her staff, James, who was demonstrating 9:00-5:00 behavior. As they were working for a small consulting company, they depended on everyone to pull their weight. She was clearly disappointed with James, as she and others had the habit of checking emails after closing and before the morning commute. In listening for what mattered most, I thought the lens through which she was seeing this was disappointment—in other words, the *Feeling* lens. When I asked if his role required more vigilance (was it a trouble shooting or field service responsibility) she reflected that it was more a disappointment in work ethic and teamwork. She agreed: It was more a Feeling than a logical job requirement. I tend to use the orientation of the leader's energy as my first clue about the lens they are using.

Applying the Zooming Technique

Zoom Leadership fosters a multitude of creative possibilities with the zooming technique, which provides flexible Thinking and the ability to quickly draw closer to or further from an issue. (On page XX you'll find another tool, "Shining the Light.") Go back to the camera metaphor: With a camera lens you can move in for a close-up in any of the angles by which I mean whether a leader has enough awareness of all lenses—or zoom out for a landscape view. Some questions to ask yourself:

How does your perspective change if you can zoom out and see it from a great distance, a bird's eye view from 10,000 feet?

Imagine your camera lens was zoomed so close to this issue that it seemed like a bee in a flower—a bee's eye view?

Hans was annoyed that Tony had not produced the research he had requested. Zooming in, I asked when it was due. Hans realized he had not named a due date, but rather, had applied his own values structure: When his boss asks for something he does it right away, whether or not it's an actual priority.

Another zooming technique you may use is the metaphor of a map, as in the above illustrations. We have all had the experience of using an online map or other GPS device and losing the relationship between where we are to where we're going as we attempt to see the cross streets. By contrast, the local map of an area can be so precise that one can miss the context, not being sure how the destination fits in the region. Or, zooming out, a more global view can provide excellent orientation but omit essential details. For example, if you were delegating a task and you give precise rote instructions then staff might not know how to handle an exception as it arises without understanding the broader commitment (such as to customer satisfaction). Ask yourself:

What do you notice about the local Feel of this issue? If you zoom in to the impact or implementation, what occurs to you (Act)?

When you zoom out to see a larger area, the whole company or competitive landscape perhaps, what occurs to you?

Seeing the Forest and the Trees

Zooming in and out provides detail and big picture perspective. Seeing miles of tree-covered mountains naturally does not provide data on individual trees. Zooming in to individual trees and then further in might reveal some of the branches flourishing with leaves, whereas others are wilting and barren. Zooming out, the whole forest may seem healthy. If you were to study a business issue, such as morale, from too far of a distance you might think everything is fine. You may miss that some employees may be disgruntled, unengaged, or in need of attention and leadership. Conversely, you may think employees are discouraged, but when you zoom in you find that only a few very outspoken people have created this impression. Zooming in on their complaints or concerns provides an opportunity to address them.

By zooming in and out you will be able to see the forest *and* the trees. Recently I used this metaphor with Bill, a client who was trying to find a way to negotiate project priorities with his manager, Cliff. Bill was struggling to figure out what Cliff was asking of him. Cliff insists that he looks at the big picture (the forest) view, but in reality asks for a detailed update (tree level information). I reflected to Cliff that he is astute when it comes to trees (in his research lab leader role): He can see each and every root, branch, and leaf to manage the day-to-day and to problem-solve. When it came to leading, however, he needed to zoom out to align with the department's strategic direction. This metaphor resonated with him and he agreed, taking that metaphor and running with it:

I can see the bark and the bird's nest too. And you're right, I recently persuaded Cliff I should tackle my projects in a different sequence, because it more precisely aligned with his goals. I was able to explain my tasks as they fit into his, larger long-term goals.

Zooming in to the details can help make an informed decision about implementation and/or previous experience with that kind of solution. It can also limit the options being considered. Zooming out to the organization direction, strategies, priorities, and values can provide important vision and guidance, but risks failing to identify obstacles and unforeseen problems that may reveal project plan or timelines. The ability to zoom in and out is also helpful to managing up: being able to articulate strategy and vision, as well as outlining implementation steps.

The First Lens: *Think*

Most leaders I work with are valued in their organizations for their intellectual ability, so when they present an issue I first listen to them in terms of how they are *Thinking* about it. Thinking about a problem may produce great results, or it may end up in a loop that goes around in circles without resolution.

Zooming in on the first lens, *Think*, may provide a new perspective and help a leader explore an issue more deeply. If a leader's view of the issue is close at hand, or too granular, then I may ask a question that zooms out to Thinking in broader terms—more strategically or more generally.

For example, a leader may excel in analytical skills. He may have built a great career on the accuracy of his data. Yet he may be faced with an issue that demands a more broad view and a quick decision— even though there is insufficient data available. In this case, zooming out from the normal pattern of relying on detailed information may provide a perspective that enables him to make a decision in a new, albeit less comfortable, circumstance. Getting out of one's own comfort zone is important when there isn't time to consider familiar, more traditional methods. Once this approach proves successful, he may be able to generalize strategy to face uncertainty with more creativity and confidence.

Occasionally leaders resist changing their range of focus. He or she may not be ready to give up the granular view. In this case I suggest zooming even deeper with another question:

> *If the budget details this quarter are concerning and the annual view isn't helpful at the moment, what happens if you consider the monthly results, or results by each department, or each category?*

I had a client, Connor, who was frustrated that his staff did not show more initiative. As we examined one of his assessment reports (which utilized the Thomas Kilmann Conflict Model, a tool used to characterize conflict style), Connor proudly noted the strength of his competitive spirit. As we zoomed into the subject of competition—which brought the focus to Connor's relationship with his whole department—he realized he was competing against his own staff. This newfound awareness inspired Connor to zoom out and refocus the department's competitive spirit, as well as his own, from going after each other to targeting the real opposition, the competition.

Another client, Peter, was productive, but had high turnover in his department. I suspected that he was either over-focusing on a task or not providing sufficient focus on relationships. In 1964 Robert R. Blake and Jane Mouton developed the Managerial Grid Model, which outlines five leadership styles. Depending on where a leader falls on the grid, he or she may over-focus on a task or relationships. Zooming in on task, Peter was proud of his accomplishments and successful attainment of goals. Zooming out, he realized his company was beginning to examine turnover as a management success metric.

Peter may not be immediately able to change his longstanding practice of focusing on task-related outputs, but he was able to envision the camera zooming in on relationships as *part of the task* he was responsible for achieving. Translating this to the Zoom Leadership technique, his *Thinking* was that his competitiveness was his strength and his *Feeling* about it was pride. Once he zoomed out, his *Thinking* shifted to the collaborative efforts of the team—which now included him—and his *Feeling* reverted to satisfaction over having changed his perspective, resulting in a culture built on teamwork.

A colleague who is very rational and logical told me this story about his family. He and his wife had one child. About eight years later, his wife wanted a second. It didn't make any sense to him. From his point of view, this was not a logical choice. Yet he became comfortable with the idea over time, as he realized that her happiness was extremely important to him. If having another child were to make her happy, then it was a reasonable choice. "The way I thought about it," he said, "was that her being happy made sense to me." He changed his perspective and they worked together to adopt a child internationally. His rational, logical decision-making was satisfied by his deeply personal commitment to his family.

The Second Lens: Act

The second lens is *Act*. Leaders may be talking about an action they have just taken or are about to take. Action may come before or after *Thinking*. The impact of that Action provides new information. Leaders may benefit from considering zooming out, taking a larger Action—or zooming in, to choose a smaller one to start.

Leaders may want to zoom into action, increasing their working speed to shorten the time line. (See more about time line on page xx). On other occasions they may need to zoom out of the time line, taking a longer time to action or imagining a longer time line for the impact. They may only need to act with their direct reports, invest in influencing other departments, or engage with their general manager in a new strategy or process.

Let's take a fairly common dilemma, such as when a leader needs to spend more money than planned. If a leader is facing a budget variance to complete a task, she must take Action. This might mean one of the following: asking for approval to increase spending; moving ahead without needed resources; scaling back the project's goals; reducing the ability to achieve goals; or spending what's needed and dealing with the consequences later. She may be so focused on delivering upon her agreement with her manager that discussing her options with her manager becomes unattractive. Consider the following:

> *Let's zoom out. What are the risks of not [taking the action of] adding staff or infrastructure? What possibilities occur now? How does that inform the risk analysis, or cost/benefit analysis?*

> *Let's zoom in to rehearse [the Act of] asking about revising the budget to still meet the project outcomes.*

> *Now let's zoom in to the Act of* **revising** *outcomes. What do you think of the above two Actions now?*

In other situations Action comes first, and the impact provides opportunities to observe the results and rethink options. Action may come first for any number of reasons. In a crisis, a leader often must make an immediate decision. Or, a leader may be experienced in handling a non-crisis situation, such as a contract negotiation, and know where she stands without a lot of thinking—so action then comes before extensive Thinking.

Publicly held companies have been famously criticized for their focus on short-term earnings. They zoom in to meet the forecast, improve quarterly results, and meet shareholder expectations. They are incentivized to view their business in a short time frame, affecting decisions and actions taken. This shortened time line may pressure companies to avoid investing in long-term capital equipment or long-range research and development, both of which could result in negative consequences down the road. In this case, leaders may believe they don't have a choice about which actions to take.

Leaders may benefit from zooming in to take a smaller action or zooming out to take a larger action. For example, when a layoff is being considered, some leaders choose to make few cuts to staff, hoping that the cost reduction of some salaries will provide needed financial relief; they have zoomed in to take a small action. Other leaders operate on the zooming out theory with the idea that ripping the band aid off once will be disruptive and painful, but hopefully at least the gains to the bottom line will be felt right away and the hit to morale will be over all at once (instead of dragging on with additional layoffs later on).

Zooming in to take immediate action sometimes results in leaders being tempted to call a meeting of their whole team to address a problem that is really with one person—for example, project lateness, quality control issues, or missing deadlines. Taking Action—such as holding a meeting—Feels like progress because the leader is visibly doing something to solve the problem. In this instance, zooming out to consider the impact to the group will save the leader from diminishing his or her own credibility. The group likely knows the intended individual who is at fault for the problem and will resent the group scolding. Another potential outcome is that the person with the performance problem may incorrectly assume that someone else is the target or that many others are responsible for causing the issue along with her.

Sometimes leaders put off making a decision because they are missing information, and therefore postpone taking action. Not all the data is in or available. Since that is often the business situation today—there are many variables that can't all be known, including overwhelming available data, product recalls, etc.—at least some form of action is needed.

> *Let's zoom out to look at several possible actions. If you zoom in to Action A, what are the possible outcomes, risks, and rewards? If you zoom in to Action B or Action C, what might be the impact of these options?*

In this way the leader has the opportunity to rehearse the actions and impacts, without having to implement them all. Practicing Action scenarios can move a leader out of indecision. (Note that this is the kind of visualization experiment that enabled Albert Einstein to discover the theory of relativity. He imagined taking an action, first chasing and then riding on a beam of light.)

These examples are not meant to imply that business issues are simple. They are not. There are multiple contingencies, dependencies, criteria, competing commitments, and unknown futures. Taking Action is related to Thinking; it is artificial to separate it, but at this stage we are presenting it as a separate view on the lens for purposes of introducing the technique.

A colleague in the wellness sector, Noah G. Press McIntyre, recently started offering a program entitled Green Leaves and Gratitude. His experience was that too often his clients became overwhelmed at all the actions required to be fit and healthy (exercise, vitamins, diet, nutrition, meditation, etc.). Instead, he helps them make progress by zooming in to take action on just two things: Green Leaves and Gratitude.

The Third Lens: Feel

As mentioned, many leaders most identify with their intellectual prowess (*Think*) and action steps (*Act*)—the first two steps in this technique. However, more and more awareness of the impact of emotions (*Feel*) is being introduced over time. *Neuroleadership* research—a form of leadership blending brain research with development techniques to make better leaders, developed by Dr. David Rock—as well as the groundbreaking research conducted by Daniel Goleman in his books on emotional intelligence—supports the notion that leaders must be aware of their emotions and be able to manage them in order to be effective and successful. Managing emotions is "self regulation," not denial. Denial or repression may be the old method of managing emotions in the workplace. That process omits a valuable source of information—that the leader needs emotional intelligence in order to build strength and alignment with others. (It's also important to mention that denial can come at the high cost of free-floating anxiety.) Emotions explored within the privacy of a coaching engagement or a one-on-one conversation with a trusted advisor can be useful to help someone discover clarity. Expressing emotions provides an opportunity for reflection and rehearsal, so the leader can connect with the threat or values breach that created a strong negative Feeling. The leader can have the opportunity to reenter his working environment with better coping skills to handle these emotions.

Often a Feeling of frustration or exhaustion is what is most visibly obvious when a leader is grappling with a problematic issue. However, he or she may not yet be clear enough to talk about the Feeling. Consider the following inquiry:

What matters most when you Think about your disappointment (or outrage?)

Sometimes the key underlying cause of anger is not being recognized—or not Feeling like a valued player. Other Feelings may include grief or loss following a layoff or reorganization or after losing a valued coworker or client.

Some organizations have a process in which leaders receive what is known as *360 degree feedback*, in which they receive confidential insights about themselves from peers, bosses, and direct reports. These can be on-line assessment where people respond to questions along a scale of 1-10, or it can be more anecdotal where a consultant speaks to colleagues, staff, bosses, and clients for impressions and examples, aggregating the responses. It is common for high-achieving leaders to Feel upset about their identified problem areas, as there is a mismatch between their perceptions and those of others with regard to their best skills and areas of improvement. This can open the door for growth or stymie leaders, depending their capacity to consider and integrate the feedback.

We can regard a 360-degree feedback process through the zoom in and out lens. A useful 360 zooms out, gives a big picture of the leader's contributions, strengths, and growth areas. It provides an overall view of the alignment or gaps between self-perception and the perceptions of others. Zooming in provides anecdotes and details that illustrate areas of focus, which are more useful than a numeric rating. Other times, 360-degree feedback is so focused on the details that the leader cannot get a good overall view of where she stands. Sometimes highly regarded leaders leave an organization because of this, because the process left them with a sense of uncertainty and no guide to help them digest sensitive, personal information. For this reason I recommend that the 360-degree feedback process only be used when leaders have the benefit of an external coach to help interpret the information and put it all in context.

To a certain extent, the goal of soliciting and processing feedback *is* to take it personally so that improvements may be made. If the wound becomes too deep, however, it can prevent the learning that is possible while zooming out. One way to accomplish greater learning is to explore the Feeling of disappointment or hurt—and then zoom in, deeper. Ironically, this kind of self-reflection can provide solace as the leader has identified the issues, considers the underlying causes for the impact, and experiences the depth of reaction. Another way to encourage learning and improvement is to just pick one or two areas that seem to matter most—or the ones the leader has the most energy to explore and develop. By initially zooming in on just a couple of priorities, the process becomes less emotional and overwhelming.

Occasionally, leaders who receive 360-degree feedback will zoom too far out, blaming the negative feedback on circumstances outside of themselves—rather than taking responsibility to address them and ownership to improve. In my experience, it is high achievers who take feedback to heart and spend emotional energy on understanding it and applying the learning. Those who do not take it to heart eventually inure themselves to the feedback and stunt their ability to grow, locking themselves out of the opportunity to provide greater value to their organizations, direct reports, peers—and even their own careers.

If the leader is ready for some self-examination, I will recommend zooming into the uncomfortable Feeling, rather than fleeing (which can be the first impulse). Those uncomfortable Feelings often contain rich and useful information. I want to help a leader find out what's at stake, what really matters. If feedback comes across as an insult, it's important to explore, zooming in on the source of the Feeling I may ask:

What value is related to that? What is most problematic? Is it fear of being regarded as incompetent? Not being liked? Is it resentment at not Feeling known? Is it having intentions mischaracterized?

Those questions all lead to different insights and potential actions. Once a leader has zoomed in and explored these uncomfortable Feelings, he has more information and therefore an enhanced ability to respond, develop a skill, or create a new impression.

By following that increased awareness—as well as naming and articulating the feeling—it becomes a good time to zoom out. Otherwise, the uncomfortable Feeling can drain energy and motivation. Scenario planning (*Thinking about Acting*) is one option. While zooming out of the hurt Feeling, leaders can consider what Actions might change perceptions—even if they believe they were unfounded. Or, zooming out of the hurt can return a leader to the overall sense of resilience and well being, equipping him to commit to developing new skills. We can explore, zoom into Action A, see if that would Feel authentic, and then hypothesize whether that might change impressions. Scenario B might be to arrange an informal partnership with a close colleague, who could privately share unbiased insights into whether the new Actions have been successful at creating the leader's intended new impression. Scenario C might be to consider whether the leader is willing to approach those who gave feedback and share what he is going to work on first. While this is a vulnerable conversation, it is also outstanding role modeling for being willing to learn—no matter how high level the leader may be. Time line zooming (see page xx) can also be useful while in the grips of a strong Feeling:

If you look in your past, are there other times you received this kind of feedback? Is it in a consistent pattern, or is it a new impression?

How do you Feel right now?

How do you Feel as you imagine yourself one month from now, looking back on this event?

Another issue that I find troubles leaders is when they are dealing with a performance issue of a staff member that has not been addressed over the course of many years. This inaction can come from a number of potential Feelings about the employee's potential reactions to the feedback. Leaders may fear that all of the energy trying to address the problem won't be worth it. There is apprehension that the efforts will fail to produce performance improvement. Leaders may also have a reluctance to devote limited time and attention to something that will not be personally gratifying or satisfying. Looking down the road, a leader may already dread the idea of searching for, interviewing, choosing, and ramping up a new hire. Yet sometimes these situations can be addressed and turned around when the leader zooms in to the reluctance—and then zooms out to the payoff. In the case of delivering employee feedback, zooming in to the feelings of reluctance may reveal important information about whether there has been a fair opportunity for performance improvement, or whether there is a risk in keeping the employee. Zooming out to the payoff may reveal the possibility of performance improvement, or the possibility of a more skilled new hire. Either the employee will take steps to improve or you will be able to set the stage for moving on to replace the staff member with someone who fills the role better. In many cases of consistent poor performance, other people in the department and elsewhere in the organization have been seeing the poor performance go uncorrected for a long time and Feel resentment toward for not having it addressed. Shifting leaders' focus from *Feeling* to *Thinking* and *Action* improves options and choices about next steps. Thus their Feelings of frustration can be an important source of information.

The value of zooming in to negative Feelings was demonstrated at a workshop I conducted at a Nurse Practitioner conference. The nurses spent some time complaining about the time-consuming aspects of a new computer system that was required to store and process medical records. They uniformly resented the extra time spent after hours to learn the program and input data. They objected to the inability to make personal notes in the system that would help bring a patient's personal situation more clearly to mind. After zooming in to the Feelings of frustration, we explored the underlying values. Once they defined their concerns as resulting from a commitment to quality patient care instead of just complaining about a new system, they remained annoyed and exhausted but were more grounded in their resilience and self-regard having explored their Feelings in greater depth.

The workplace can also be source of positive emotions for leaders, whether it's the joy of digging in to a hunch, collaborating with others to improve a new idea, or seeing someone benefit from mentoring. Even joy can be marginalized in companies—but it is the fuel for innovation, so it's worth zooming in on it!

Leaders can use their awareness of *Feeling* not only to inform their own position and values, but also to learn more about staff and what is going on. Leaders can use this same technique when helping the staff cope with a pending merger, for example. When it comes to guiding team members through their reactions to situations like this, leaders can help them dig into the related values at risk (such as continuity, familiarity, confidence, and gratitude for the past). Identifying and acknowledging Feelings increases the chances they will be integrated constructively.

Another opportunity for leaders to help others with Feelings is following the loss of a major client or prospect that seemed like a sure thing but fell through. These losses can send a company into fear mode, interfering with the very skills that are needed to survive and thrive during the threat: resilience, productivity, and innovation. Leaders can guide their teams to zoom in and face those fearful Feelings, explore them, and own them. Then they can zoom out to share the overall history of success that the company has previously experienced, reassuring the team with evidence of long-term stability.

The Fourth Lens: Witness

Occasionally, a leader's concern, distraction, or sense of being unsettled has to do with a bigger sense of purpose. Perhaps there is a yearning to leave a legacy, or make a different kind of contribution in another area (such as becoming a mentor or a leader returning to more hands-on research). Sometimes there is a deep disappointment about being thwarted while trying to play a bigger role. In these cases, the person may benefit from the solace provided by an attentive listener, bearing *Witness* to her larger calling. It may be beneficial to first zoom into the disappointment in order to explore the meaning of that sense of loss and grief (*Feel*). Later, she can zoom out to the larger vision, the sense of being inspired to manifest her personal mission in a different role.

For example, a devastating layoff or termination can leave a person without his usual sense of mooring. Being fired from a job—especially if a leader believed all signs were positive—can crack the foundation of confidence. One colleague, who built a board by encouraging members to refer others, ended up ousted by the board. A coalition of assertive board members who previously knew each other banded together to replace him based on a disagreement over vision. He had worked hard to build the management team as well as the board, and saw the termination as a betrayal of his professional relationships with them. Zooming in to the Feeling of betrayal and loss—including a future he had worked hard to create—was part of his healing. Zooming out to appreciate his own contributions over the years enabled him to rebuild his confidence. My role was merely to bear *Witness* and encourage him to do the same: to gain some distance and see the time with that board in a broader context. This enabled him to get past the hurt, and assimilate the learning.

I once met someone whose business collapsed when her computer hard-drive crashed and she had no backup. She took the opportunity of being at the ultimate bottom to recreate herself. She Witnessed her own disaffection for the old business and her surprising relief that she was forced to rethink how she was going to earn a living. She Witnessed her own reaction—zooming in to her sense of tedium—in a way that enabled her to quickly move from shock to mobilization, zooming out to new possibilities.

A non-profit leader who survived a vote of no confidence later realized that her interests and the needs of her constituents were not a match. She spent months disappointed that she was misunderstood and not valued for her considerable skills. She felt her efforts were marginalized and her strengths disregarded in the face of her weaknesses. This reflection—this Witnessing of her own experience of disappointment—later provided the energy she needed to leave the organization and, after some months of volunteering, retreats, and workshops, refocus her career. She zoomed in to her initial relief that the board kept her; zoomed in to her disappointment with ongoing complaints; and zoomed out to her own personal larger vision, which mandated that she not compromise her greatest gifts. While acknowledging she had weaknesses, she chose to find another organization for which her strengths were a better match. She Witnessed her own cycle of loss, disappointment, victory, relief, and resolve.

Sometimes a person has to think out loud in order to work out his or her issues and access inner wisdom. In that case, a supportive leadership coach, mentor, or friend who is an attentive listener can bear Witness. It can be extremely reaffirming for a leader to vent aloud with a trusted person to find inner wisdom; the listener may be silent or provide gentle reflection. When Witnessing this process, the listener remains in the present before offering any kind of timeline or prediction. In our fast-paced, action-oriented corporate world, mindful listening can be undervalued but it makes an enormous contribution to the leaders struggling with reflection.

Time Line Zooming

Time can feel subjective when it comes to both positive and negative events. A rare visit with a cherished friend feels fleeting, even though it lasts for hours. When caught in a cold rainstorm without a coat or umbrella, you are likely to feel that a 20-minute walk home seems to take forever.

This trick of time also varies by the perceiver; the same event may seem entirely different to two people. The first snowfall each winter in New England brings special delight to me. No matter how many harsh, snowy winters I have experienced, that first seasonal snowfall is magical—even though I realize my perception will change dramatically after a couple of subsequent blizzards. Maybe it's the deep memory of a no-school day—an unexpected play day out of the ordinary routine. Or, maybe it's seeing the world transformed, blanketed by pure white. One year, when my son was about ten years old and the first snowfall was piling up, he came running in with excitement and said, "let's go sledding." The sled he referred to was an inflatable tube, about three feet in diameter. It had been put away after the previous winter ended, so naturally it was deflated, folded small, and put in a box along with other seasonal things. I searched in one such box of winter items—and another and another, until finally, I was able to emerge from the cellar victorious, waving it over my head. "Look!" I shouted. "I found it!" I could already feel the wind in my hair and the fun of speed in my stomach, even though the experience would be later that day or perhaps the next. My son's face was impassive. "What?" I demanded, "aren't you excited I found it?" He replied, "I'm not sledding yet." This is an example of a difference in perception of time lines. His was totally focused on the present. Mine was at some near term future.

A client once joked to me that her adult children complain that they have no sense of time and that it's her fault. When her children were young and it was almost time to leave the playground and return home she would say, "10 more minutes." From their point of view, it seemed like she had only given them one minute when she said the time was up. But she admits that if she ran into a friend "10 more minutes" became *30 more* minutes, which seemed interminable to them.

Each of the four lenses—*Think*, *Act*, *Feel*, and *Witness*—offers the possibility of being examined through an altered timeline. The impact of a decision or issue can change depending on how much time has passed. To alter the perspective on time, zoom in and out on *Thinking*, for example:

> *What do you Think is most pressing about this for you right now if we zoom into the present?*

If we were to zoom into the future and look back on this issue a year from now, how does that alter the way you are Thinking about it? What importance will it hold?

What do you Think will be the impact of adding a large new client right now if staff is already overloaded? What do you Think will be the impact one year from now?

Or, conversely, what do you Think will be the impact of terminating a relationship with a very big, but high-maintenance client?

Zooming into the short-term impact of the last question above, you may anticipate a loss in revenue and productivity. There may also be more staff on hand than is needed during that month and the next. On the other hand, you might consider the impact the high-maintenance client might have upon employee morale and even profits, especially if the client were to be unreasonably demanding. Zooming out to the long-term impact, you may have room to add other, more desirable and/or profitable clients. By zooming in you can see that closing the door on a problematic client engagement can open the door through which better-fit client may enter.

The 1993 movie *Groundhog Day*, which stars Bill Murray, famously recounts the story of a weatherman doomed to repeat one day in his life over and over until he is redeemed by learning something from his tedium. After repeating the same day with his usual cynical outlook, he finally decides to do things that help him become a better person. He is eventually transformed, gaining new perspectives about life, love, and appreciation for others. The film distorts time, providing a useful, self-reflective tool.

If you had the chance to do something over, what would you do differently?

What did you learn that might be helpful if you face a similar situation in the future?

How could you optimize the experience, even if it doesn't seem ideal right now?

Shine the Light on a Problem

Often changing one's perspective can provide the needed insight for leaders to create a solution to a problem. Drawing closer to or further from the issue offers the necessary opportunity for reconsidering options.

Sometimes, however, a problem persists even after bringing awareness to options that are closer or further away. In those cases, it may be that the focus is on the wrong issue. In addition to zooming in or out of the issue and examining it from various time perspectives, there is one other tool that can be very useful: changing the object in focus. In other words, you aim the spotlight in a new direction.

Following Donald Trump's surprise win in the 2016 U.S. Presidential election, reporters reflected at length how everyone (except Trump) had failed to predict the outcome. One major reason, journalists admitted: "We were focused on the candidates instead of the voters." In other words, the spotlight was pointing at the wrong subject.

Many leaders attempt to contribute to a solution by identifying what is wrong. We can zoom in closer to that issue or get some distance on it, trying to identify the root cause. But when neither of those approaches proves effective, it may be that the light is shining on the wrong thing. Surprisingly, focusing on what is going *well* can often unlock new insights, spark innovation, and energize the team. David Cooperrider describes this approach in his book, *Appreciative Inquiry*. Cooperrider recommends focusing on what is right with the organization (and individual) to solve problems and create new realities. The premise is quite compelling: If an organization is still around, it must be doing *something* right. When the strengths and positive outcomes of the individuals and the organization are highlighted, more attention is focused on those strengths. The result is that the staff becomes motivated to achieve more of these positive outcomes.

A surgeon named Dr. Light (yes, that's his real name) consulted about his own experiences with surgeons regarding the pain in his right wrist. As recounted in Dr. Jerome Groopman's book *How Doctors Think*, being a doctor gains Dr. Light access to specialists and knowledge; in fact, his wife is a physician as well, further expanding their personal network. Yet even with these advantages, he goes to *four doctors*—all of whom examine his right hand and retake x-rays, even though he already has them. Each specialist diagnosed the problem differently and recommends a different procedure. They all shined the light on his right hand, where the pain was occurring. Then he went to a doctor who took an x-ray of both his left *and* right hand while in the act of turning. By changing the focus of the spotlight from one hand to two—and from hands being still to moving—this doctor discovered another treatment opportunity.

Recently I attended a presentation by Garrison Keillor, host and creator of the long-running radio program *Prairie Home Companion*. While onstage, Keillor pondered the miracles of technology. With his trademark hesitation, he spoke about the voice on his GPS: "It's a woman, not my wife, giving me instructions," he said, pausing for effect, "and when I don't listen, she just says 'recalculating.'" Perhaps we have all had the experience of missing a turn, only to have our travel companion complain, criticize, or get anxious. Keillor's joke reminds us that the spotlight can move from "what went wrong" to "what comes next." How can we shine the light on "recalculating"?

In parenting, I can attest to my own stubborn focus on safety and risk management. I did not want my children to come to harm. I was guilty of trying to teach them the mistakes I had made in life so they could avoid pain, disappointment, and loss. I thought the spotlight was on them; if they took my advice, I wouldn't worry. Eventually I realized that the older they became and the closer they were to leaving the safety of our home, the more I had to own that my risk-averse worries were no longer helping them. The spotlight had to shift from them to me. I had to work through my own acceptance that parenting is incomplete, and own that the only possible next step was for me to manage my reactions.

"Don't look at the room, let the room look at you." This is a rec-ommendation from a book literally on vision, *Take Off Your Glasses and See*, by Dr. Jacob Liberman. Although I read it many years ago, there was a memorable eye exercise the author recommended which called for relaxing the eyes, covering them, breathing deeply, and then slowly opening them. "Take a minute to bring your attention within yourself. Allow it to wander through your body. Allow your eyes to close gently.... Then, as you exhale, very gently and slowly allow your eyes to open. As you open them, don't look at anything... allow the room to look at you." That meditative concept—trying less hard and seeing as the result of being a *receiver* of images—is a wonderful, counter-intuitive example of shifting the spotlight. So often our spotlight is on exerting effort, but the act of *receiving* can be a powerful shift in perception.

In her wonderful book about alternative perspectives, *On Look-ing: Eleven Walks with Expert Eyes*, Alexandra Horowitz describes how her urban walk changes based on who accompanies her—from a sociologist to a physician to a geologist to a toddler—because what they see is so different. Each companion sees through different eyes. The geologist reminds her that cement and paved roads are rock, for example, and even identifies the likely quarries that produced some stone building blocks. By demonstrating curiosity for where each person's attention is drawn, her own perspective is enriched and it changes the city in which she lives.

Paying Attention

This brings us back to attention. The things we pay attention to can change the look of the entire landscape.

In business, my clients often begin by "wishing things were dif-ferent" and that "others would be different." In one week I heard several clients in a row lament, "why don't they *think* like me?" They were kidding—but only partially. As long as the spotlight is on the other party, there is no opportunity for resolution. The spotlight needs to shift to the self, engage in possible new behaviors, and puzzle through the benefits of considering ideas that are foreign or even seem ridiculous. Leaders need to question inferences they have been made and absorbed as fact.

Sally Taylor, daughter of famed singer/songwriter James Taylor and Carly Simon, has a YouTube video in which she discusses "Essences"—a game her family used to play. In it, one player thinks of an individual. Then the others ask: "If this person were an animal, what might he be? A vehicle? A food?" But the real fun, she says, comes afterwards, when players disagree with the characterizations, offer up different foods or vehicles, and everyone learns about others' perspective. In this talk, she also references the parable of the seven blind men and the elephant—each of whom is sure he is describing the elephant accurately, while the others are not. The one who touches the tail is sure he's feeling a rope; the one who touches the leg describes it as a pillar; the one who touches the ear is sure it's a fan. The reality in the parable is that each has a partial truth.

One client shared with me the progress of two new hires who worked for her. Their spotlight was focused on correcting procedures that were clunky. The manager agreed the procedures were clunky, but *her* light was focused on the big picture—the whole system (and a longer time line)—and she was not willing to implement band aid solutions until the employees had three months of experience. She felt they needed a more extensive knowledge of current processes and an understanding of the ripple effect of their recommendations. Their light was shining on the quick fix, while the manager's spotlight was on the strategic long-term solution. She was willing to endure a couple more months of the old system while the new business and computer process supporting it were being finalized.

Ira, a prospective client who worked for an engineering consulting company, was discouraged that his new initiative had stalled. He described his frustrations about the company to me. Other partners had become frustrated with his lack of progress, but when pressed for a clear statement about what they wanted, they were not clear about what success looked like for this initiative. Almost as an after-thought, he added that the two founding partners, who had run the firm for more than 30 years, had passed away in the last year. The partners' light was shining on Ira's initiative and its lack of progress, when perhaps the focus needed to be on assimilating the dramatic changes the whole firm was experiencing. The spotlight on initiatives concerned *Action* not taken; the spotlight on the founders' deaths were about giving the staff an opportunity to *Feel* (grieve).

Leaders who are not satisfied with results will frequently encourage or direct staff to be more productive, work harder, and put in longer hours. There can be diminishing returns on long workdays. Many of my clients realize this and plan an offsite for an entire day or two, where fun is mixed with long-range planning to address such problems. While there is certainly time spend on business strategy and concrete Action steps during a retreat, an important benefit is shining the light on play and socializing—not only work and productivity. There are times when the spotlight needs to shift from work ethic to renewal and fun interaction. No amount of zooming in or out of productivity issues to gain new ideas on how to work harder will restore staff, if what is really needed to boost morale and productivity is *play*. The book *Play: How It Shapes the Brain, Opens the Imagination, and Invigorates the Soul*, by Stuart Brown, M.D., makes the case that play is good for imagination, energy, and innovation. Play disappears if there is not enough food or sleep, but as soon as those needs are met, play reemerges—which means it is a core human need. Moving the spotlight from work to play can paradoxically increase productivity.

A client engaged me to work with Brenda, a director responsible for large complex projects. Often my engagements are focused on coaching newly promoted individuals who have taken on more significant responsibilities. My client insightfully realized that Brenda was a burnout candidate; she was working hard and putting in long hours. My coaching engagement was designed specifically to help her achieve balance (meaning: work less). Her entire department could recognize which days she exercised: She was calm, focused, and constructive. On mornings in which she skipped her beneficial exercise routine to get to work and accomplish more, her productivity was actually lower, as was the morale of her staff.

Another CEO client told her hard working executive staff, "I want to see you staring out the window." In other words, she knew that the benefits of reflection would pay off in terms of renewal and productivity. Her spotlight did not have to only be on *Action* steps. Rather, encouraging them to *Witness* their own inner thoughts would manifest meaningful results.

Now that I have explained the fundamentals of the four lenses of the Zoom technique, let's explore its application in leadership at work.

2

Lens One—Think

Leaders rely on analyzing, comparing, researching, remembering, and engaging in cognitive activities. Planning, strategizing, and scenario planning are all necessary and beneficial to successful leadership.

The first lens, *Think*, is essential for leadership success, although there can be a downside as well. Leaders who spend too much time on Thinking while performing their tasks may become involved in unhelpful activities like perseverating—focusing on something uncomfortable, disappointing, or threatening over and over. This process can include anticipating a negative outcome and then forgetting that it's a hypothesis.

At its best, Thinking provides important data, options, and reasoning. Sometimes Thinking can get too close to the details, obscuring the broader implications. When this occurs, zooming out is helpful. Sometimes Thinking can focus on big opportunities and possibilities, without the leader considering whether those plans can be implemented and executed. That's not necessarily a bad thing. Successful entrepreneurs notoriously agree that they had no idea what they were getting into and, if they did, they may not have jumped in with both feet. For those with entrepreneurial ambitions, thinking big without a lot of detail can be an essential element to advancing a unique business concept.

The ability to *think critically*—a necessary trait for every leader—includes the awareness of the Thinking process itself: biases, influences from previous experiences, and beliefs that are so ingrained they are difficult to see. Critical thinkers must be willing to challenge themselves to reduce potential distortions and increase self-awareness of motivations and predispositions.

Research in the neurology of leadership demonstrates the impact of new ideas on cognitive function "when participants were exposed to others' ideas, stronger activation was detected." New and original ideas are fun and stimulating. Thinking out loud together enhances the exploration of creative possibilities. Big ideas that are shared generate more ideas. Thus zooming out to the big picture is extremely beneficial in the creative process. Zooming in to the details to consider implementation steps and challenges is a thinking process that results in focus. Both are needed.

Below are some examples of conversations in which leaders changed their focus of Thinking, increased self-awareness, and identified new ways of thinking about issues, all of which resulted in new creative approaches and solutions.

Bill—Delegating and Developing

Bill was a team leader responsible for his own work and for supervising other software developers. He worked on a different floor than those who reported to him, so he didn't supervise them a lot. However, he knew that he had a reputation for being unapproachable, and became concerned that he did not hold people accountable. In my experience, these two issues could be intertwined.

J: (Janet): Bill, what is your priority for our session today?

B: (Bill): I know I have a reputation for being too detached, unapproachable. I don't really feel that I am, though I can be abrupt if someone interrupts me when I'm focused. But it's an image I'd like to change. I think I am approachable, so it bothers me. I don't know where to begin.

I notice that he has begun with an analytic problem. It's a way of thinking, and the thinking it through is his priority. Even though he also has Feelings about this, I'll start with the Thinking.

J: Give me an example of this kind of interaction.

B: Chen came in yesterday and hesitated, saying I looked really busy. And honestly, what he wanted me to review is tedious to me, obvious to me. I have other things that are more urgent. More interesting. So I do make it a lower priority, to review his work. I could see that it seemed like I was giving him the brush-off.

J: In that moment are you thinking this is tedious, or even unnecessary? And that you're in a hurry to finish something else?

B: Right.

J: So what did you do?

B: I gave him a few tips, verbally, and followed up with some more specifics in an email.

J: Did that work?

B: I don't really know—but I don't think it helped my unapproachable image issue.

J: If you had spent time with Chen, you figured that there would be a cost—it wouldn't really be a learning experience for you. Would there be any longer term payback in that scenario, following the cost?

B: Well yes...reviewing his material feels forced and bureaucratic—micromanaging even.

Bill is zooming in on the downside of working differently with Chen and yet he wants to create a different reputation. Not ready for the payoff.

J: Anything else?

B: Yes, like I am not trusting—not trusting him.

I'm thinking Bill is zoomed out a little too far on the managing and monitoring spectrum. Leaders who want to treat their staff respectfully and professionally sometimes back off too much. The result is frustration on both sides. Staff members don't Feel they are learning or getting quality feedback, and managers end up being puzzled and disappointed that more work has not been accomplished.

J: Answering questions does take time away from your other work. These are all legitimate concerns, and common ones for approachability and delegation.

I'm Thinking about his perspective on time. Like most of us, Bill is focused on what needs to be done right now. A new perspective on time might help him achieve what he wants. I'm going to have him zoom out.

J: Let's imagine that it's a year from now. What would you want Chen to be able to do that he can't do now?

B: He would be more proficient in the programming language that we use. He would keep me better informed of milestones and he would be the lead on the project we are doing for Michael.

J: And what would be the benefit to you?

B: Well, I could take on more interesting projects. And I would be more confident when I delegated to him.

J: And what's the cost of that to you?

I'm still responding in his Thinking mode, even though there are Feelings of confidence mentioned.

B: It would take more time and attention in the short term—but if I keep my eyes on the prize of developing him, then I would remember it's worth it. That would bring the payoff to mind.

J: What else is in the way?

B: Well, it's hard to delegate.

J: What is your thought process when you try to identify a project to delegate?

B: I'm thinking, "I can do this faster and better—it will take more time to explain it than to do it." I give my staff projects but they come back for more details on what I want, or they don't get to it, or they take too long. And I feel responsible for the result. If I do it myself, I know the quality and I can feel comfortable that my responsibility for a good result has been met.

This is a classic delegation dilemma, the result of being over focused on the short-term productivity goals—which sometimes is the right business decision. But this doesn't develop others or build the team's competence. I'm Thinking it's time to zoom out again from the current moment to the long term, asking

*a question that could either be about Thinking or
Feeling.*

J: And when you think of that, that you can do it
better, why would you want to change that and delegate more?

B: I keep doing more and more—and it doesn't solve the
unapproachable reputation I have. And I eventually get
resentful about how much I'm doing.

J: If we bring your attention to a year from now, what
would you like? What would be happening then that is
not happening now?

B: They would see me as a good manager and mentor.
They would be able to take on more kinds of projects.

J: What do you think would be the result of that?

B: I might keep them longer and have less [staff] turnover if they felt like they were continuously learning.
And I might be better able to spread out the work, not
do so much myself.

J: This doesn't ensure that it will be easy going, to
change the habit of not delegating.

B: I know—new habits are hard for me.

J: But bringing a focus from very near term to longer
term provides a framework for considering options.
How does this relate to the accountability issue?

B: I tend not to follow up. I don't think I should have
to, I guess, and it's the thing about not wanting to
micromanage, or to seem that I don't trust them.

*I'm Thinking that the focus is too far out. Bill has
drawn a conclusion that Chen may make about his*

motives. It's time to zoom in. To accomplish this, we explore an example of a project Bill delegated and then found out two months later that another team member, Jean, was way off course. Bill's attention has been too far away from the interim progress for him to meet his own goal of holding people accountable to results and time-line.

J: What would it take to stay closer to the projects you delegate?

B: I used to have weekly one-on-one meetings. I guess it's time to resume that. I admit, I wasn't that good about keeping the meetings. If I had a deadline related to my own work, I tended to reschedule until I was completely out of the habit of meeting with him regularly.

J: What if we looked at regular meetings with staff— overseeing their work, monitoring progress, and keeping them on track as falling into the category of "my own work." How does that change the picture for you?

This zooms out the focus of what counts, so that the work of his team counts as "real work."

Bill thought out loud about how he could refocus in two areas. One: He would bring himself closer to his team's progress on projects. He thought weekly was too often, so he contemplated meetings every other week. If he missed a meeting, he would be more intentional about what he called "walkarounds," casually checking in to see how things were coming along.

Two: Bill would try on the new focus—that is, instead of his spotlight shining mainly on his own individual work, he would include managing and monitoring in the spotlight of what he considers *real* work, his work.

Often managers like Bill—who have their own individual-contributor work, in addition to management work—don't count "management" as *real work*. Refocusing or zooming out to widen the lens (or aperture, to use camera language) provides a new view. Now he can experiment with a fresh perspective and include the responsibility of the whole group as part of his responsibility; then it becomes part of his real work instead of something he gets to later. It brings a new focus, and enables him to give *himself* credit for an activity that is much harder to measure: developing others. It is harder to measure, but done well developing staff brings a level of impact in unseen areas, including engagement, productivity, performance, and career growth. This development effort has greater leverage than any one leader can create on his or her own.

Malcolm's Culture Fit

Malcolm, a new hire, was a savvy, skilled, confident, and capable leader. His new employer recognized these traits, which is why he was recruited. Malcolm was highly educated and knowledgeable in his tax accounting niche, and had a reputation for creative approaches to projects. He had been at his last employer for 18 years and wanted another lengthy stint.

His manager, Richard, brought me in to coach Malcolm because he was not fitting in with the accounting firm's culture. He was actually annoying and alienating his peers and professional staff—people he had to work with closely. According to Richard, Malcolm was so smart, capable, and sure of himself that he did not recognize that he came across as arrogant or that he was flaunting culture. His new company was more collegial and collaborative than he was accustomed to. Although the company valued his expertise and wanted him to work out, Richard felt that his behavior was becoming an issue that raised doubts about his long-term potential. He talked too fast, too much, and too forcefully.

> J (Janet): Malcolm, Richard has a high regard for
> your expertise and is quite pleased you joined the

organization. What has he discussed with you about working with me as your coach?

M (Malcolm): Well, I know my directness has been an issue. In my last job, they understood me—knew I was being efficient. I don't waste a lot of time on needless conversation. I get right to the point. That's good for the client—and for all of us.

J: And how is that received in your new company?

M: Well, as Richard has told you, people here don't get it. They don't get my contribution. I can be blunt, but I'm just coming straight to the point.

J: Anything in the way besides your bluntness?

M: I'm not getting the kind of credit and recognition I'm used to, that I've always earned by my great solutions. I'm creative. I think of things outside the box, and that creates innovative solutions for clients. But sometimes I lose people when I introduce an unconventional solution.

While Malcolm is mainly presenting from a Thinking perspective, describing what he knows, when he describes the criticism, and comments about insufficient credit it is a clue that we will also need to consider Feel as a lens.

J: What happens when you lose them with one of your creative ideas?

M: They push back before I have finished describing the outcome. Mostly they don't realize how much I know about these deals. I'm willing to share what I know, but people won't listen. I've heard that people think I'm arrogant. But there's nothing wrong with being knowledgeable and confident—and willing to share.

J: What do *you* want to be different?

M: People shouldn't complain that I'm arrogant or bull-dozing other people. I'm not.

Malcolm has demonstrated important awareness of the current situation. His first lens in this conversation is the Thinking orientation. His analytical straightfor-ward, creative style has previously created long-term career success. Zooming in on his Thinking, I want to verify his goal.

J: So perceptions about your intentions are something you'd like to change?

M: Yes.

When senior managers change jobs, they are often surprised and baffled by the new culture. Most orga-nizations cannot name it or prepare a new hire. They learn the hard way: by annoying or alienating the people in the new "tribe." I want to zoom out to Think about this cultural context with him.

J: I know you were successful for many years in your prior role and were sought after by this company. Would you like a new perspective on what might be happening?

M: All right.

J: You may just be going at a different pace than the norm here. Do you have any Southern relatives?

M: I do—I know where you're going with this. They all talk slower than we do. And move slower.

In order to zoom out and take in a broader cultural context, I highlight that the tension may just be cultural, and I share a recent exhibit I had seen at a museum. Thousands of years ago, elaborate sandals were the marker of the leader rather than a jeweled crown, which literally turned status on its head.

J: Right. You have a different, faster pace of thinking, and a different pace of speaking. And you have knowledge not widely shared among your peers. You've said they don't understand you. In some cultures, the king is the one with the grandest shoes but has no crown. The cultural norms here are different, perhaps upside down to you.

Zooming out in this way helped him get curious about the culture. Being unaware of the new culture's norms didn't make him wrong. There were no travel guides to the new land. His spotlight was on his expertise, so I broadened the focus in a way that reduced his defensiveness and increased his curiosity. The only guidance for the new culture is the feedback he's getting: awareness of what triggers negative reactions in others, increased awareness of his own habits, and testing new approaches.

M: It's not so much that things are wrong with me, as the perception others have. I do have some anxiety about all the balls I'm juggling.

He is already experiencing the implications of a culture shock, but zooming out of the complaints about him to the broader view enables him to connect to his own Feelings about this.

J: What about the anxiety?

M: I know I'm capable. I've always been rewarded for my smarts. I'm successful. How can I help it if they don't get it?

Time to zoom out from what I'm regarding as a combination of Thinking—why don't they get it and Feeling hurt.

J: Capability, smarts, success, all of that can fit here. How do you see success?

M: Being the best in my field—and being clear and direct and forceful about it.

J: What else is being asked of you now?

M: (pause) My interactions, I guess.

J: What if you expanded you view of success to include the interaction with colleagues?

*He was Thinking he was communicating efficiently and directly, and I zoomed out to include the **impact** of that habit on listeners. It's simply a broader spotlight, but a big shift for someone who has used one set of criteria for success, and now finds that being challenged.*

M: I could try that.

I now zoom into Act.

J: What would that look like?

M: I think I'd sometimes have to bite my tongue. Say less. Listen more.

J: Anything else?

M: I don't know—make sure they know I know what they're saying. Thinking about all this makes me feel like I've had too much to drink. It takes so much concentration.

I'm Thinking that, based on the anecdotes he was sharing, this is probably how others were Feeling about speaking with him: It takes too much concentration. Or he makes them Feel slightly off-balance. Now I want to zoom out to the longer view.

J: What would make it worthwhile to exert the effort to work in these different ways?

M: I enjoy coming to work. I'm proud of my work, and the money I make. I am super at what I do—the top 5% in my field. I don't want to leave. It's a prestigious firm.

I note that these are all pretty strong motivators.

A few weeks later, after checking on his progress and new approaches, I brought up another goal his manager had mentioned to both of us...

J (Janet): How are things going?

M (Malcolm): Mixed. Sometimes the reactions I get don't make sense. When I don't understand them I do what I call a "Malcolm lobotomy." I ignore that part of my brain that noticed the other person drawing the wrong conclusion—reacting in a crazy way.

J: Does that help?

M: Yes, I am trying to manage my conversations, be more precise. The other day someone stopped in and asked a question. I was about to launch into a long explanation. But I stopped myself. I said, "You don't want to watch me make the sausage."

He zoomed out of the detail.

J: And did that work?

M: As George Bush would say, it avoided the risk that he would mis-underestimate me.

J: How does the fact that you replaced Peter [the retired predecessor] affect you?

M: They worship at the altar of Peter. Whatever Peter did was great. Which doesn't make sense because I hear that he was really arrogant. Arrogant is what they complain about, about me. I don't get it. But I've learned that they worship at the altar of Peter. So when I hear that, I do a "Malcolm lobotomy."

I wouldn't have used that metaphor, but it is a way of zooming out of the feelings of confusion or resentment.

J: What are other ways you gain perspective?

M: I tell myself, "Never attribute to malice what you can attribute to stupidity."

J: What do you want now?

M: I'm going to pick off people one at a time—win them over one at a time.

This zooming in to build relationships one at a time is an effective strategy. Culture can be so hard to decode, that strong individual relationships are a great place to start.

Adjusting to a new culture for an experienced and confident leader poses a challenge. It requires two seemingly opposite strengths: one is to bring knowledge, expertise, and confidence; the other is to be curious about, and "not knowing" about, the new cultural environment. The leader must be willing to be a trainee in that regard and be able to reframe the pushback he's receiving as separate from his competence; this is key to being able to integrate the two dimensions. As his defensiveness reduced, he could modify his delivery and style of communication, and still use his intellectual prowess to contribute his area of expertise.

Keith—Department Dynamics

Keith was responsible for an Information Technology department. He was interested in spending more time designing the service offerings of his department, including more prevention-oriented programs, which would include efficiencies for users in the organization and among his own staff. At the same time, he was pressured by his manager, Sam, to work on the details within his department. Some of this was because Sam was concerned about the reputation of Keith's group.

> K (Keith): The challenge is we need to manage the expectations of our internal customers. I see the value of our group at a higher level than Sam does: We can anticipate issues, strategize efficiencies, and automate routine functions. I also need to be clearer about expectations of my own staff.

> J (Janet): Do you think there is confusion among your staff about expectations or scope?

> K: Yes, and partly that's because there is confusion among our stakeholders. They might go right to my staff, and they don't know whether they should solve the problem or pass it on to someone else.

> J: What's an example?

> K: Recently, Walter [on his team] ran into a stumbling block with a hardware problem. He felt it was not his issue, which is accurate. But he didn't escalate it didn't let anyone know. He just did nothing. That's not the right action.

J: So communication is an issue?

K: Yes, we need better communication. I've tried a lot of things, but I'm not sure we're there yet. I want to have them push information up to me, but sometimes I have to pull information.

J: What have you already tried?

It sounds to me like he has made a clear analysis of the situation (Think) and has a clear goal in mind. I need to know where the spotlight is now, and where it has been.

K: We've tried department meetings, which is all right to let people know what projects we're working on. But each person does such a different job that it's not that useful to come together as a group. Usually only one person is working on a given project.

J: What else have you tried to improve communication?

K: We've come together after a project is completed, and reviewed what worked and what didn't. I want to be sure we learn from it.

J: That sounds like a good opportunity to improve processes, as well as individual skills.

K: In a way—but I'm so sensitive to individual styles, a group is more difficult for me.

J: Let's explore that a little. What are the individual styles in your group of four?

Before having him zoom out, I want to zoom in with Keith to his perception of each person because it's useful to highlight his insights and it's a comfort zone for him. He is alluding to an issue of Feeling here: his skill at being sensitive to individual styles and his dis-comfort being able to keep track of everyone's Feelings in a group meeting.

K: Manny is precise and detail-oriented. He's quiet and keeps to himself. It's hard to draw him out, but he's a hard worker and his output is good. Stephanie is more expressive, outspoken, and upbeat. She's a good thinker at a high level. Not as detail-oriented, but scopes a project well. Glen, I'm worried about. He can take too long on something, doesn't come to me when he's stuck, and doesn't seem to show initiative for researching on his own. I'm not sure how to put the ball in his court more consistently. He'll follow a precise outline but can't problem-solve if an issue comes up that's outside the norm.

At this stage I want him to zoom out to the group as a whole in order to have an altered perspective.

J: Now, imagine that you are just there to watch the conversation—even before you take on responsibility for managing the group meeting or adapting your style to make each person comfortable. Imagine that you have a drone with a camera flying above them. Just for a minute, let's say that you are not responsible for the content of their conversation. What do you notice about the conversation? How are they speaking towards each other?

K: They're friendly enough, but they don't really engage with each other's content.

J: Great, so you have identified one dimension of what we can call their "group dynamic." Is there something that you would like to be different about it?

K: Most projects involve just one of them. But I'd still like to see them interact. I'd like them to acknowledge each other—what they're working on. Respond, ask a question even. Update each other on changes to equipment or a challenge from one of our users [internal customers]. It may affect them down the road and, in the meantime, they'll be learning from each other.

J: Okay, good to know. So even though you are more comfortable one-on-one because you are sensitive to individuals, you do have awareness of what you would like to see in the group.

K: But I don't want to mandate it; I don't want to sound preachy.

Keith has zoomed out from the focus on the group dynamic, a dimension of Feeling, to the potential management impact on the group and perceptions by the group. He has valuable self-awareness of these dimensions of Feeling—wanting to create a change without imposing it.

J: It sounds like you want that discussion to be collaborative. So let's explore ways that you can lead a conversation and that encourages participation—about encouraging participation! In fact, it's a perfect opportunity to role model the exact dynamic you would like them to learn. At that level, what else would you want their group style or identity to be?

Now I'm creating an opportunity to move into Act—or at least, considering options. Until now, Act in this issue has been to try a few group meetings, and then stop having them.

K: More inquisitive, more preventive-oriented. Con-sultative. I'd like them to do more outreach with our users. Not just fire fighting.

He has effectively zoomed out to overall goals (Think). Now let's zoom back in to Act.

J: Okay, given that and your preference for having this be an exploration with the team, how would you like to engage them?

K: I don't know.

By now it was clear Keith was Thinking about what was wrong with his team. I want to change the focus to what was right *with the team. In other words, have him shine the light in a different direction.*

J: What do you think about starting the next team meeting with: "What is working well here?"

K: Hmm...I'm not sure that will get me what I want, but I'm willing to try it.

He is shining the light on a new area. He is now willing to Act and see what happens.

Our next session was two weeks later...

J: How was your team meeting?

K: I was a little concerned about your question about starting the group meeting with "what are we good at." But it really worked. It was a different kind of meeting, focused on who are we.

J: How did you engage them?

K: I asked them, "What are we good at? How do we know we're successful? What can we do to be more successful?" I was concerned at first, but then quite surprised at how effective it was. It kicked off a good discussion.

J: It sounds like they had a lot to say?

K: They really did. I successfully engaged the group.

Even though it is a bit counter-intuitive to begin with "What is working well?" when the leader is focused on what needs to improve, these words can open up a new dialogue. Often the focus on appreciation reduces the anxiety level and invites participation. By concentrating on what is working well, it invites participants to articulate what they have not previously noticed because it was in the background. It also provides a shared experience or even vision and a stronger foundation on which to grow, experiment, or try new things. Keith was able to move from Think (analyzing the problem) to Feel (know what was bothering him) to Act (try a new approach).

Donna—New Boss

Donna has been in her job about a year, and has initiated coaching because the company and her department will be growing. Her primary goal is to foster teamwork, while at the same time maintaining accountability and providing feedback to her staff. In addition, she has been working without a boss all of this time and now has a new manager, Marjorie, who just started a week earlier.

J (Janet): So what do you want from our session today?

D (Donna): Well, I'm a little worried about Marjorie starting. I've been used to running my own ship here—not that I don't have to meet people's expectations. As head of sales engineering, I have lots of bosses: the sales department, and the marketing department. Really all of management cares about us successfully closing prospects. And then there are the prospects who have demands and expectations. So I've had plenty of input on goals—I just haven't had a day-to-day boss.

J: What are you most concerned about?

D: That she'll limit my scope, rein in my responsibilities, or mess with my staff.

Donna has zoomed into the future. Sometimes doing this to alter the time frame can be useful speculation, but isn't usually productive when it causes stress without supporting data. Even though she starts with her worry (Feel), she seems to be presenting logical, factual information about the company and the department—the Think lens. I want to pull her zooming into the future back into the present, through a Thinking lens.

J: Since you don't yet know how that might change expectations, would you like to discuss your strengths and contributions, so that you feel articulate and prepared to update Marjorie on your past year?

D: Yes. I know I'm conscientious, organized, and a big picture thinker. I have also accomplished a lot. *(She names several projects.)*

J: Great, do you know anything about Marjorie's style?

D: So far, I have seen her be kind of vague—it's too soon to say. I know this is a bigger job for her than her last one. I also know she never managed managers before—in fact, she never managed anyone with more than a high school diploma. We're a big, prestigious company. She could even be insecure.

This is useful that she has zoomed out of her own reaction into what her new manager's experience might be.

J: Is there anything that you'd like to develop besides acclimating to a new boss and building your team's skills?

D: I also have an issue with one of my staff, Jessica. She doesn't finish projects, then goes on and on with excuses. I can't stand that. I just cut off her explanations and excuses.

"Cutting her off" is an understandable thought, but not usually an effective management response for changing behavior in a way that engages an employee or improves performance. Time to zoom out.

J: What would you rather have her do? When she begins to explain why something went wrong, what do you expect from her instead?

D: I want her to pull her weight, take responsibility.

J: How can you describe to her what that would look like?

D: I want her figure out why it happened—get to the root cause. Create new processes to make sure it doesn't happen again.

That sounds like useful perspective. Zooming into the future in a preferred scenario can help her back up and Act in a way that will affect that change. Also, zooming in to being more concrete about her expectations—such as identifying root cause and new processes—will be more useful to Jessica.

J: What would that look like?

D: I want her to manage her relationships better. Help network internally. That makes everything run more smoothly. It will help with the image of the group. I want Jessica to partner more with our internal customers to help them design what we should deliver.

It's good to be clear about expectations. Let's see if I can shine the light on any strengths, any skills that Jessica brings.

J: What are you satisfied with in terms of Jessica's performance?

D: She is conscientious, has materials ready on time at meetings, keeps track of who shows up, and her presentations appear to be well organized.

J: Have you told her that?

Building off strengths helps a leader engage staff. From a practical standpoint, we all learn best from a solid foundation of something we already do well.

D: Not in so many words. I get so frustrated that she blames others. But I've told her she needs to shape up.

That kind of comment is not useful; it's too zoomed out and judgmental for most listeners. I suggest she zoom back in.

J: Can you concretely describe your expectations and what milestones will help her achieve them?

D: (She describes projects and deadlines that she will more clearly articulate).

We wrap up with Donna planning to acknowledge Jessica's strengths and for Donna to be more specific with expectations, including due dates and milestones. Donna realizes it will be challenging to develop this new habit, but sees the potential payoff.

At our next session, we return to the issue of the new boss...

D (Donna): Marjorie is driving me crazy, flip-flopping. I told her that. I know she just got here, but what the heck does she want?

This kind of directness with a new boss can create untended consequences. I guide her to zoom in to the irritation first (Feel).

J (Janet): What is it that is most frustrating about her approach?

D: I don't know where I stand, I don't know what she wants, and I don't know how to succeed.

This sounds like there is potential for overwhelm. I want to zoom in to have her Think about one thing.

J: Let's take the first one. What is an example of not knowing where you stand?

D: I told her I wasn't satisfied with Jessica's performance. I told her what Jessica does well, what she doesn't do well, and why I'm not willing to keep working with her. She called for a meeting with the three of us, telling me that she intended to back me up. Then, in the meeting, she sided with Jessica. She said Jessica was credible, liked by her colleagues, and a capable presenter. I told her I want to fire her and she said she'd back that. Now Jessica's great. So, which is it?

J: Can you find out what Marjorie values in Jessica?

D: It's so hard to read her, figure out what she thinks is right and wrong. She has so much underlying emotion, nothing is predictable. I have to disregard what she says.

Zooming in to confusion, Donna is describing (Think) the dynamic with her manager. However it's possible to zoom in to the facts and contents of what she says and disregard the inference, which is speculation. The Feeling of frustration may be coming from inference rather than concrete information.

J: What did she say?

D: She said Jessica gets good ratings from others. That she's new and wants to be fair. And that Jessica seems genuine.

I'm wondering if this has to do only with Jessica or if there is a dynamic between the two of them. Let's shine the light on that relationship.

J: On other topics, what do you notice about your inter-actions with Marjorie?

D: She said that I sometimes talk like I was saying "f*** you" to her. Other times she's friendly and asks me to lunch. Was I looking at her like, "you crazy woman"? Possibly. I don't want to get into the swirl, so I stayed calm—but I was infuriated.

Zooming from Donna's Thinking lens to the Feeling lens her manager is expressing can send one swirling. Deal-ing with what is is the starting point.

J: What could you do to connect with her when she is unpredictable like that?

D: Well, I could just let her rant and draw her ideas on the white board. Even though I don't agree with her direction—and she'll be expecting me to implement the project plan—it would be helpful to know her thinking.

J: What might happen if you were to ask her, "Is there anything I can do that would help?"

D: Yes, I can do that. I'll try that for now, although I'm not sure Marjorie is someone I can work with for long.

Sometimes zooming in to another person's perspective on Feeling can create a better connection than remaining calm while they are agitated. If we zoom in on Thinking, the main goal here is for Donna to get along with Marjorie long enough to assess whether she wants to stay.

J: Job #1 is to build rapport with her, not solve the problem of the [project]. You've said that Marjorie likes to mentor. She finds satisfaction in that. Is there some area where you could invite her to mentor you?

D: I have to think about that. I'm not sure she knows enough to mentor me.

J: Can you ask Marjorie to weigh in on your project—for example, ask her what might be important as an end result to this project and which stakeholders she says are key contributors.

D: Yes, I can do that.

Donna is used to relying on her competence and commitment. Time to zoom out to not knowing.

J: Can you wonder about what's important to her?

D: Working with Marjorie is like watching a cartoon. She is so exaggerated.

One of the most toxic aspects of a relationship dynamic is Thinking about negative judgments. Donna has negative judgments about her manager's skills and inconsistent decisions. Her manager may have judgments about Donna's being on board with her goals, or Donna's skills at drawing out the best in her staff. Flexible Thinking, or reframing, may help Donna develop new strategies with her new boss. It's possible that even after trying new approaches, Donna may Think that the divide between her skills, job goals and values, and her manager's priorities and communication style cannot be bridged. Flexible Thinking opens up opportunities for learning new ways of Thinking, but it cannot always resolve differences.

Evelyn—Urgency

Evelyn was responsible for community outreach in a healthcare network. Darren, Evelyn's manager, described her as positive, energetic, focused, insightful, and adept at relationship development. Darren was eager to develop her as he saw even greater potential for Evelyn's future beyond her current role.

One goal in Evelyn's development plan concerned urgency: She needed to exercise more discernment, rather than treating everything as equally urgent. Urgency is a great skill that is important to preserve while other skills, such as prioritizing and weighing options, are added. Another goal was to raise awareness about a strategic view. Evelyn was a strong advocate of whatever was on her mind; she was motivated by a competitive spirit, but sometimes took Action before considering the ripple effect. "Everything has to have a strategic purpose," Darren reminded her.

Evelyn and I began by discussing her manager's feedback. She was growth-oriented, which Darren wanted, but he needed that view to encompass the whole organization. She had strong advocacy skills, but tended to present only one recommendation to address a problem at management meetings. Her manager and the management team were looking for her provide more options, so they could be better informed about her assessments and weigh in on the recommendation. They had a collaborative work culture, and other managers could sometimes feel left out due to the speed at which she spoke, made decisions, and took Action. They wanted her to consult with them, and reflect that she had considered the impact of her recommendations on other departments and the whole company.

J (Janet): What do you think of this feedback?

E (Evelyn): If I see a problem, I know it needs a plan. Often other groups are involved. We may all have small steps, but need to plan for progress to meet the time line. A lot of things—even outside my department—come to my attention. I know it needs a plan. I do jump in.

J: What do you like about that?

E: I'm high energy and I know I get a lot done because of that. But I am ready to move out of my comfort zone.

J: In what way?

E: One small way is for me to be more comfortable with silence. I know I tend to jump in.

J: What would help that?

E: For one thing, see if I can wait. And see if I can think about what their thinking might be—without jumping to conclusions. Stay open.

J: Do you recognize times when you are comfortable with silence?

E: In my personal life. In those instances I know people. I know where I stand. I'm comfortable with them and they are with me.

Evelyn strikes me as a clear thinker. It sounds like she has given these things a lot of thought. I'd like to zoom in to what she is Thinking to see if she is aware of her own thought process.

J: Can you eavesdrop on your mind when others are quiet at work and hear what you are telling yourself?

E: Ha! How did you know I talk to myself? Well, usually I'm thinking that they are quiet because they aren't agreeing—or they are getting ready to rebut.

Zooming out a little, since that way of thinking is limiting her response.

J: Is there another way you can think about this?

E: I can try to be a blank slate. It's hard for me to slow down, but I know if I didn't make up what they were thinking, I could tolerate their silence better.

She has clear Thinking about that. I'm zooming in on other her other thoughts about her goals.

J: Where else do you want to step out of your comfort zone?

E: I know I'm judgmental. I can jump to conclusions. Sometimes when people do things I think, "Why don't they know this isn't appropriate? Don't they have common sense?"

J: Does that reaction interfere?

E: Well, I know that I can carry that judgment—that I can let it carry over into my next interaction with someone. And, in that way, sometimes it does interfere with me really hearing them.

She has awareness of her Thinking, and of the impact of that on her Actions, her interaction. I'm wondering if there's any Action she wants to try. Let's shine the light on Action.

J: As an experiment, what might you try to do differently when someone's really quiet?

E: *(laughing)* You ask hard questions.

J: That's my job!

E: Focusing, I guess. Focus out the window or on the report we're looking at. Maybe count silently. See how long it is.

J: Can you try that out?

E: Yes, I can try those.

I know I don't have the full picture yet, so I want to know more about her Thinking.

J: Is there anything else you want to do, to get out of your comfort zone?

E: Challenge myself—accomplish more. What do I mean by that? I'm not sure. What would give me a sense of more accomplishment? I like working on new things.

J: What new things seem appealing?

E: I'm ready for growth, ready for a change. I wouldn't want a boss who doesn't tell me what I need to learn. I'm 47 years old and working on my master's degree. I figure I have 15 years left—maybe more. But it seems finite. It didn't used to. I want to accomplish more. I want a lot I am not currently doing here. I don't want to travel so much. I don't want to go to so many industry shows and community meetings. It makes grad school really hard. I'm not just driven by money. I like working with a team. It's important to be with a team that's excited about the same things. I can't stand negativity. I want to be upbeat and be with others who feel the same way.

Even though there's a Feeling of frustration, her energy seems to be analytic and intellectual, so I want to zoom in on what she knows about what else she is Thinking.

J: What are the values that you care about, the ones that aren't being met?

E: I value professionalism, honesty, accountability, and trust.

I want to know more about the underpinning of these values, zooming in on her thoughts.

J: What are you most proud of?

E: Developing my team. What about it? It was a challenge. It was new and different. It evolved, I evolved. I took the team from a small place, worked with them, and developed their skills. I developed their strengths. I'm really proud of that.

J: It sounds like that was really satisfying—what about that is meaningful for you?

E: The other day I got an email from Ralph. He recently transferred out of my department to another one here. He said I was the best listener he ever worked for. He said I would give him the direction—where we were headed and then the specifics. He said I listen and can be objective. I know I can help others do that. I'm not as good with being objective about myself. It can be hard if you've never been exposed to being challenged like that. I'm more uncomfortable with silence. But tell me everything, challenge me, and I'm fine.

I think she skipped over something. I want to hear more about her Thinking.

J: Can you say a little more about not being as objective about yourself?

E: I do get invested. If I have a good idea, I want to run with it. When people challenge me, it slows me down. I don't mind talking more about it, but it can seem personal—until I get my bearings.

J: Great. What helps you get your bearings?

E: Oh I don't know. Remembering people just want to be a part of things. And that they are challenging the idea, not me. And that they want to make a contribution, just like I do. I want more influence. If I have a good idea, I want to present it and get support.

J: Darren is very supportive, which is something to consider for our next session. Are there ways you could influence the design of your role? What would you like more of or less of?

Evelyn is pro-active, which resulted in her many promotions. The way she Thinks about obstacles is very take-charge, and that has benefited the organization. Her manager is now asking her to Think more strategically, take in the needs and priorities of other departments, and Think more collaboratively. This is a common stage up the promotional ladder. For many years, people only have to keep their direct manger happy in order to get raises and promotions. At a certain level, often at Director or Vice President, more points of view are required to be successful. The same Thinking about urgency can still be beneficial, as long as the lens of key factors includes issues and processes that may be urgent to others. Thinking and Actions need to include the ripple effect: the impact on other departments and potential future consequences. Flexible Thinking strategies help a leader acclimate to this new job requirement.

Daniel—Thinking Partner

Daniel is a software engineer in a medical device company. We had just finished meeting with his manager, Karen, to define goals due to his recent promotion. He was managing five people, and now manages fourteen people. Four of those are direct reports who manage the others. It is the first time Daniel is managing other managers, but he has been with the company for eight years and is well regarded—both technically and as a team player. Karen is sympathetic to the cultural challenges: "People are pulling Daniel in all directions. He is responsible to me and my manager, to his direct reports, his internal customers, product development, and design. On top of that, he considers feedback from our users. And we rely on him to communicate his progress to the entire organization. I don't need to know everything that his department is doing, but sometimes I get surprised that one of his team members is being used by another group, or that someone has suspended work on a project. I don't like being surprised. I should know how resources are allocated. You can get pushed down a path by a senior leader, when that path isn't our priority."

J (Janet): What did you think of that meeting?

D (Daniel): It's true. I can be led down a path by important people.

J: What would you prefer?

D: I'm pretty clear on priorities—but still, I need to be responsive to leaders. Not just politically, which is important, but because they have strong opinions about direction. I don't really know how to reduce their influential pressure.

J: What do you think about when they ask you?

D: I just think, "Go do it."

J: How can you tell they're not just thinking out loud?

D: Well, good point. I may take an inquiry to heart, like it's a directive. I've always been susceptible to that kind of influence. Hey, I've been here a long time because I try to keep people happy—do my projects, create good solutions, and accommodate requests.

Daniel may have a belief about being accommodating that has developed into a habit. It's common for a manager to take an inquiry from people higher up the ladder as if it was an order. Executives sometimes don't realize the impact of status—especially when it's a culture that seemingly values open door policies. They can be thinking they are being collegial—kicking around possibilities—whereas others can hear it as "go do it." Daniel's automatic response to accommodate has served him well up until this point. What happens if we Zoom out of that Thinking?

J: Daniel, can you think of an example where an inquiry turned out just to be that—a discussion, and not a new requirement or deliverable?

D: Yes

J: What would help you remember to verify whether it's an inquiry or an outright request?

D: Hmn, well, bringing that example to mind. And also another one where I *did* implement what was being asked when it wasn't really being assigned to me. That really derailed us for a while, and it cost my group a lot of time. It was pretty embarrassing, really.

I'm considering shining the light on the inquiry. What if he was able to be a leader or a partner in a conversation like that—even with a higher up executive—instead of just implementing?

J: How might you show up as a resource in a conversation like this to find out whether you are the order taker or the thinking partner?

D: Oh, I like that. That would be kind of fun. I don't know. I haven't really played that role in an informal brainstorming way. I mean, I do when the meeting agenda is to brainstorm new products, but when one executive comes to me I don't know. I don't think of guiding the conversation.

J: What would feel comfortable and genuine to you in trying that out?

D: Well, I do have a lot more nuts and bolts background about software development, and by now I have a fairly clear idea of our products and customers, so I could start by just making sure I know what he's talking about—what he hopes to accomplish. Then I can share my experience with other products that have or haven't worked out well, as points of reference. Maybe use the old "compare and contrast" approach to guide the conversation and find out more about his thinking.

J: Does that seem like something you'd be willing to explore?

D: Yes, depending on the person. Some seem to be willing to challenge and debate. Others want compliance and cooperation. Or, at least I think they do.

J: Well, that's an important distinction...that assessment and awareness of the different players.

D: Just by updating them on all we're doing—they may not know the related projects to the extent that I do. Just sharing that knowledge and how they link to this new idea would be worth trying.

J: That sounds to me like it would add value. What do you think?

D: I think we need to be able to figure this out. There's an art to us telling them what to ask us for. And exploring outcomes. Otherwise, it becomes a problem if a new demand is made too late in the process. At the beginning, maybe we could push back more. Not in a refusing-to-do-it kind of way, but just in verifying criteria and outcomes. If we don't explore and make it clear in the beginning, then revisions take a long time and our internal customers end up even more disappointed.

J: What do you think would help?

D: Part of the problem is that we need to hire first class software engineers, but that doesn't mean they know mechanical engineering or biology. The temptation is to think we just need to be really good at software— but then we can make the wrong decision about the approach.

J: What are you thinking about changing?

D: It's not just those extra skills. It's a challenge, really, because we don't want to be too hierarchical with how people approach us with projects. We want to remain flexible—but then it does happen, like Karen said, and people end up deployed on projects she doesn't know about. Sometimes even I don't know. Also, there are more concurrent projects than ever.

I'm noticing that Daniel is used to being more in the details and, now that he has broader responsibilities, he has appropriately zoomed out. But maybe it's time to get closer.

J: What would give you more control—or comfort
that you were up to speed on projects and resource
allocation?

D: Clearly I need a better project plan: a listing of
projects people are working on and the status of those
projects. I need to make sure I know their deliverables... and that list will be a deliverable for me. Beyond
that, for each of the fourteen people, I want to work
with supervisors to identify what is pivotal: a strength
to leverage, a better sense of that person's motivation,
and skills they need to learn.

Daniel's success has been due to his "just do it" approach when
his leaders or members of the senior team ask him for things. He is
now being asked by his manager to modify that can-do attitude to
be more strategic and aware of his group's projects and milestones.
He finds the alternative of being a Thinking partner to be appealing.
It is still a way to be responsive and engaged, and it leaves open the
possibility that Thinking together or brainstorming is all that is being
asked of him. He can then explore that possibility without feeling he
necessarily needs to take immediate action. Flexible, fun, open-door
cultures particularly run the risk of inadvertently burdening staff by
engaging in impromptu discussions. The remedy is simply to clarify
the conversation. Maintain that culture and define what is a wild
idea vs. what is a specific request. One idea-generating entrepreneur
had a particularly bold staff member who would growl back at the
fifteenth assignment in twenty minutes, "is that a requirement, a
question, or a SWAG?" That communication style may not work in
many companies, but such flexible Thinking—that a comment may
have any one of several meanings—can be quite helpful. Daniel was
willing to challenge his Thinking pattern to come up with several
new approaches.

Often when leaders are faced with a challenge they first rely on their analytic Thinking skills. When this usual approach does not yield a satisfactory result, new insights can be gained by focusing closer or further from the issue. Simply changing focus begins to introduce flexible thinking, even before a new insight is achieved. Simply rethinking the *range of focus* may loosen rigidity and begin to open creativity.

In Bill's example, his deep focus was an asset when involved in his own problem solving, but a liability in his management role. Expanding beyond his usual (and successful) habit of deep focus opened up new ways for him to manage.

In Malcolm's Culture Fit, he had brought his previous learning about culture, without being able to see it. Most of us cannot see the culture we are in. Culture consultants often use the expression: "Do fish see water?" to illustrate our unawareness of culture. Recently a colleague referred to culture as a "stew." That illustrates the changing nature of it, and that one new ingredient can alter the whole. In Malcolm's case, his Thinking had been focused on his expertise; he needed to readjust to take culture into account.

Keith, in his Department Dynamics scenario, was Thinking at a high level about what his department could offer, and at an individual level regarding staff's assignments. What he needed to add was a focus on the dynamic interaction of the individuals, so that he was not in a spoke-and-wheel formation the only one in the group with information about the others' projects.

Donna's commitment and critical thinking skills kept her productive and well regarded during a long period without a direct boss. She had become accustomed to that level of independence, and struggled with the limitations and expectations of a new manager. She understandably had a strong investment in her projects and areas of responsibility. A new perspective may or may not be able to salvage the challenging relationship, but flexible thinking will add to her skill set wherever she goes.

Evelyn was a good, clear thinker and had been rewarded for that over the years. She had a restlessness I would describe as entrepreneurial. She was capable with her department, but came across as territorial—not a senior level team player. Her challenge was simply to change the range of focus to include other departments and the whole company.

Daniel overreacted to senior leaders' inquiry, taking them as directives or mandates. This responsiveness had been good for his career, but was starting to interfere with long-range commitments. He needed to track his projects and find a different way of participating when new possibilities were introduced.

3

LENS TWO—ACT

Action comes naturally. When faced with a dilemma, we take steps to explore whether an action will work or not; this is a core human ability.

For many of us, work requires concentrating and taking actions to produce a result—to be productive. Still, some actions can be taken out of habit—even when they don't yield optimal results. Gaining a new perspective on actions to take (or not take) can open up vast possibilities.

Taking actions that are considered experimental are also effective ways to explore possibilities. Scenario planning is a way to Think about Acting.

Leaders can Feel pressured into action by a sense of urgency or client demands. When leaders are not comfortable with the urgency, choosing a smaller step can yield new data to help assess the viability of an Action.

Taking the long-term view can better inform a quickly needed decision and possibly reveal new criteria. For example, leaders with a vacancy understandably Feel pressured to recruit, interview, and hire talent. That pressure can compel a leader to make a hiring decision based on the short-term pressure. Some leaders have shared their regret at hiring candidates who primarily knew the industry, only to find out later they didn't have sufficient depth in the job skills. Other times leaders who care deeply about culture have hired on candidates with deep job skills, only to discover later a culture mismatch that was not sustainable.

Leaders often talk about wanting their staff to provide innovative, creative new approaches, which can be difficult when under pressure. Zooming out from serious results to playful brainstorming or inventing can provide new possible Actions.

Shifting the focus from taking an Action aimed at productivity to taking one for the fun of it may paradoxically yield better results. Author Stuart Brown, M.D., investigates this in his book *Play: How it Shapes the Brain, Opens the Imagination, and Invigorates the Soul*: "Companies want to talk about [play] because many corporations rightly identify play as their most precious commodity. Production matters now, but creativity is the source of all growth—the new products, new techniques, new services, and new solutions to old problems mark the difference between a company that will thrive and one that will soon be deader than the eight-track tape.... Play is the mother of invention."

Nora Protects Her Staff

Nora was a fairly new manager within the accounting department. She had recently been promoted by her boss, and they had a good rapport. She and I had been working for a few months when we had this session. Nora had a problem, and she came right to the point: She wanted to figure out what to *do*, how to Act differently.

> N (Nora): I really like Roger, who works for me—but my boss, Susan, doesn't like him. Or at least, she's got issues with him. That puts me in the middle. Not only that, it's really obvious to everyone around here, and

people keep coming in my office to talk about it. Everyone can see they are *at* each other.

J (Janet): Do you know how to respond to that?

N: No, not really. I don't like that it's out in the open—as a matter of fact, I don't like that this problem is even there.

J: How do you feel about Roger? Do you agree with Susan's assessment? Do you want to fire him?

N: No, I don't. I've already invested a year bringing him up to speed on our accounting procedures and software.

J: So you feel he's making progress? That he does the job well?

N: Yes, I'd hate to replace him—but I can't stand the pressure of being in the middle.

Nora is talking about her Feelings and we could have explored that further, but my sense was that she recognized how uncomfortable she felt—and why. She needed some options on how to Act differently. First I needed to zoom in to get more data, and make sure she was clear about her facts.

J: Then it's clear something has to change. Maybe he's not getting the message about what that is. Tell me, what do you like about him? What else does he do well?

N: Co-workers and internal customers like him. They like him because he is responsive, personable, and accurate. He checks his work and his numbers are good.

J: That all sounds good. What are Susan's objections?

N: She thinks Roger requires a lot of micromanaging, so he didn't lose track of tasks. She says he's not very proactive or good at initiating projects, and she doesn't like his attitude.

Attitude is tough to articulate, manage, or change, and people generally disagree with another person's judgment in this regard. Still, I wanted to zoom in on what Nora saw as Susan's data.

J: What is it about his attitude that is problematic for Susan?

N: Roger is too familiar with Susan. His style of speaking and relating is casual, as if they were two buddies getting a drink. When he's in on department planning meetings, Roger will push back on assignments. He'll explore the relative merits with Susan about whether he should really have to do certain things. Susan sees that as debating. She doesn't want him to debate about assignments. I've seen Roger do it. Susan does not feel she needs to justify her delegating decisions.

J: Anything else?

N: Roger interrupts Susan in meetings. He interrupts her during the day when he has a question if I'm out, rather than verifying availability or saving questions for the next scheduled meeting. He disagrees with Susan on priorities. He talks over her. He makes inappropriate jokes in the middle of a work-related discussion.

Now that we have shined the light on Susan's different perception, I think it's time to zoom back in and get some more specifics on Nora's experience. She will have more overall information than her boss.

J: This is really different from how you describe him interacting with other people. Now that you've said what Susan objects to, which you've seen, what have you noticed about his manner and attitude with others?

N: He uses good eye contact for in-person meetings with co-workers. With his peers he checks for scheduling availability. When he needs to interrupt for a comment or question, he first apologizes and asks permission. With internal clients' new requests he schedules callback times and summarizes his understanding of the inquiry or request. He follows up and runs reports. His voice tone is friendly and patient, including with vendors.

J: Those are all good strengths. Have you told him?

N: I think he knows.

I'm Thinking the issue is that for some reason Roger had Susan in a different category. When Roger's focus was co-workers or internal clients, he demonstrated appropriate communication skills and behaviors—all of which comprise what we might call "attitude." He needed to move the focus, widen the camera lens and zoom out in order to move Susan into the client arena and treat her as if she was another department head.

J: What would change if Roger regarded Susan as if she were the head of another department—or even as an outside vendor?

N: Hmm. Well, those people all have good things to say about him.

J: How might you do that?

N: I like the "catch him doing it right" approach. I often will see him or hear him with others. I could use that as an example. Tell him it's a kind of spreadsheet template or formula and he could use that same formula with Susan. That would make him laugh, too. He's a little geeky that way.

Nora understood that once Roger zoomed out of mistaking Susan for a friend or acquaintance—and instead zoomed out to where Susan was in the client part of the mental map—that he would have access to his natural strengths. Nora had discovered an Action to take to reduce the tension between her supervisor and direct report.

Lee Learns to Delegate

Lee had been with her company a long time—nine years—and she was only 38, so in many ways she had grown up there. She was in a senior role and had handled a quality control function all on her own until the company grew to a staff of thirty.

Lee was conscientious and, since she knew more than her staff about the quality standards and history of products, she ended up doing a lot. She took her work home on a regular basis. One of her goals was to delegate more and develop her staff, so that she didn't spend so much time as an individual contributor. She had a tendency to do as much as she could and, for the most part produced good results. She did get overwhelmed, however, and lost track of some commitments—which occasionally disappointed people inside and outside of the company.

When we first started working together, she wasn't sure how she felt about management. She had succeeded in parsing out parts of the job to two other experienced people in her group, who were pretty self-sufficient and proactive. Beyond that, when management became more challenging—such as orienting new hires or meeting with staff when their results were disappointing—she tended to go back to what she did best: her individual contributor work. She acted independently and did not Feel as productive when her Actions were oriented towards managing her staff.

J (Janet): What would you like most to focus on today?

L (Lee): Oh I don't know. My vacation was pretty good, but all this work was waiting for me when I got back. I knew that would happen, so I would log in to work emails in the morning. But I wanted to get away and take a real vacation, so I didn't do any work the rest of the day.

J: Great, what enabled you to do that?

I'm looking to convert her awareness of her taking time off during vacation to other areas. We zoom in to her internal Thinking about really taking time off, which may help her reach for it more often.

L: I don't know. I think it was pure exhaustion. We had a deadline before I went and I had a new hire. I just didn't have it in me to do a lot of work, so I asked my staff to take care of things.

She delegated because of her Feeling of exhaustion. So I'm zooming in.

J: I'm hearing that exhaustion worked as a motivator. Is there some way you can delegate before exhaustion happens?

L: I do want to continue to move into more oversight and management. I like getting my hands dirty and really digging in to the work. I'm really good with people I've known a long time. I can read them and adapt to their styles, even when I'm telling them I've found a quality problem in their product. Sometimes I do a Vulcan Mind Meld—you know, that *Star Trek* trick of sharing minds. I can tease some people. With a few people I have to be direct. With others I need to be indirect—or very careful.

J: Sounds like that relationship skill is also a theme today.

L: I like that part, but I deal with some of the same issues over and over. I'm not learning.

J: It sounds like you place a really high value on learning.

L: Right, doesn't everyone? What's the point if you're not learning?

J: What else is working, besides exhaustion, to help you move towards your goal of delegating more and putting yourself in a position to learn more?

L: Well, I'm trying to draw a line in the sand of what we handle. It's a jagged line, to be sure. I used to pick up the ball and run with it. We have to get the work done. I'm not talking about ignoring other people's needs or operating like an island where I'm only concerned with my own group. I'm willing to pitch in, and I'm always going for good quality because that's going to keep us a good company. But I'm starting to say, "Here's what needs to get done, who would be best to do it?" That's new for me. Instead of just taking it on, I need to be willing to ask others if they will own it.

She is using a Thinking lens—thinking about drawing a line in the sand—as well as a Feeling lens (exhaustion). Now I'm focusing on how she wants to Act differently and why because that's where the energy seems to reside.

J: So you're clear on your motivation, and you are trying a new approach. How is that working?

L: Not that well. In addition to bringing my own staff up to speed, I have to teach people in the other department what's gone wrong and how to prevent that, or we end up having to clean up their mistakes. So I'm training people in another department. Sometimes one-on-one, sometimes with their managers.

In a way she is zooming out, paying attention to the overall organization effectiveness, which is well-intentioned, senior level Thinking. But taking responsibility for other departments keeps her locked in to her old pattern. It's time to zoom back in to how she can Act in her sphere of influence.

J: How can you enroll those managers in training and preventing problems, as well as post-mortems, rather than doing the training yourself?

L: I had a meeting the other day with people from my group and software development. We were reviewing software bugs. I have been over this before. It's not our job to train the software department. Better training would mean they could get better results. It's their job to do it right the first time. They think it's our job is to come in and sweep up the mess. Well, it's not. And that approach is not good for the company. It's the same old conversation we've had over and over. I'm a broken record. Why doesn't anyone take responsibility?

I am beginning to Think we are not advancing the agenda and am getting restless. I realize it's time to zoom into my own Feelings. I am Feeling unfocused, distracted, and a little unclear of our direction. I'm Feeling impatient and urgent. I Feel as if she is resisting. I am aware enough to know that what may seem like a client's resistance is a reaction residing within me. I catch myself and return to the moment. Having zoomed in to my own Feelings, I zoom back in to right now; instead of what she needs to change, I zoom in on what she is telling me she does well.

J: It sounds like you are really committed to the whole organization and making a contribution to the company's success beyond your own department. You highly value learning and recognize your effectiveness with a wide range of personalities.

L: *(Tears up)* I feel like I'm outgrowing this. I don't want to feel frustrated, aggravated. Doing the same old crap. I can feel the winds of change. I don't want to keep doing this. But I don't know what the winds of change will bring.

By having her zoom in on her strengths, it freed her up to acknowledge her fears about her future. Her Feelings. It's time to zoom in a little more to the present moment, as she doesn't yet know how she wants to influence the future.

J: It's good to know what you're considering—what the possibilities are. And that it's scary. You've embraced a lot of change before. You've told me about a move across the country, a marriage, a divorce, and a job change.

L: Yeah when you put it like that, it's true I guess. I have dealt with a lot of change.

J: There are a lot of moving parts here. What do you want to focus on over the next few weeks?

L: I guess I should start with remembering I'm resilient. I can change.

Feeling vulnerable actually helped her Feel resilient. Now I want to change the lens to Act in order to see

*what she can do to zoom in and learn more about her-
self and what her own ideas of her future may be.*

J: And then—can you collect some data about what you
enjoy doing, what you would like to keep doing, and
what you've outgrown?

The possibility of a job redesign can be both exhilarating and
intimidating. Her focus started out being too close in on the details.
Feeling overwhelmed was at the surface, and we were able to explore
what lay beneath. When we zoomed out to her big picture orientation
on the well being of the company, she was able to discover more
for herself, about what the future may hold. The future can create
anxiety, so what she can do for now is notice what she has outgrown
and what energizes her. This will provide an assignment for her and
enable her take an Action, which may bring down the anxiety. Less
anxiety will create the conditions for her to consider bigger options
and be more open and creative. In a way, reducing anxiety gives her
the opportunity to consider what still might be scary—the future—but
now tethered with more data.

Florence—Burnout Candidate

Florence, who had just turned 50, worked for a real estate development
company in marketing. Given the ups and downs of real estate development, she always felt pressured to expand the company's visibility
through name recognition and prospects. Her manager, Paul, had
recognized that Florence was a burnout candidate and, after many
years of seeing her loyal service, wanted to be sure she stayed. We
had just finished meeting with him, outlining coaching goals together.

J (Janet): What do you think of Paul's goals for your
development?

F (Florence): It's kind of ironic, isn't it, that his "development" goal for me is to work less? But I agree with
him. I think he's right. I've been feeling it more and

more as I edged closer to my birthday. I'm feeling over-whelmed, exhausted, and resentful.

She understood her own Feelings, so may not need prompting through that lens—though it may be a combination of Feelings.

J: Now that we've heard from Paul, what do you want from our sessions? Anything that you would add to the agreed upon goals?

F: I know I have to prioritize better. If I'm too distracted and try to do everything as soon as I notice it, I don't get to the important things.

J: Anything else?

F: Yes. I really do want more personal time. I love my job and the company is really great to me, but I want more personal time. I'm in an aerobics class and I always feel better when I go, though I often skip it. I just bought a cello—that's huge for me. I played it when I was younger and gave it up, but I've always loved the sound. I really notice the sound whenever I hear classical music. It sings to me. Even though I know I'll never be a professional level musician, I love the feel of it, the smell of it, the sound of it. I knew I couldn't just "find the time" for music unless I did something drastic like spend a ton of money on it. And line up a teacher.

I'm hearing a strong orientation to Acting. Besides her list of activities, the sensory details are a clue. Now that we've looked at goals, I want to shine the light on motivation.

J: What do you know about your motivation?

F: I've given up too much for this job. I gave up my book group because I didn't have time to read the books or go to the group. I gave up going to the movies, which I have always loved. This is something I wouldn't say in front of Paul, but my husband and I only fight about this job. He thinks I give it too much time, too much of myself. I'm always checking emails, sending emails. I want to reduce the tension at home about this. Nobody is making me do work this long, work this hard. I know I'm doing it to myself.

We've pinpointed the goals of what she does and doesn't want, as well as the motivation. Now I want to shine the light on the foundation—the core of the job.

J: It sounds like there are a lot of things about this job that must be satisfying, right?

F: Yes, I like being a manager. I like being knowledgeable. I like being in charge. I like teaching—the teachable moment as a manger, though I don't get as much of that as I would like because I'm always so busy. When I do, I like to include the group - let everyone benefit from learning something. This job is exciting. It's like working on the stock exchange! There's always something new, something coming at you, something really high stakes.

She sure likes the Action!

J: When I hear you describe this, there's always something you need to do.

F: There is. At the end of the day, I like the quietness. That's when I can get to things that have had to wait.

I thought she might be about to reflect on her day, but the focus is still on Acting.

J: That's when you end up staying late?

F: Yes. I need to clean things up.

Being so Action-oriented, zooming in on her own activity seems like a place to start.

J: Now that we're taking some time to reflect on this—to notice what you do, how you're currently working, and what your goals are—let's focus in on yesterday. What did you work on after 5:00?

F: (She describes a project using a software application.)

J: What would happen if you didn't do that?

F: Our records wouldn't be up to date. It takes work but there is important payoff.

J: Who else could do this?

F: No one else knows the app.

J: Is there any way this could be handled differently?

F: I suppose I could teach Liz. She's a pretty quick study with apps. But it means I would have to take things off her plate and give them to someone else in the group. In the short term, I'd have to give up some things I'm doing to find time to teach her.

J: What do you think about training her?

F: That's worth a try. I can carve out some time to teach Liz the app. I can't just say that I want more time and then do nothing to make it happen.

J: What else do you do after hours?

F: I return phone calls to others who have input into a marketing project.

J: Who else could do this?

F: I like the relationship part. I've gotten to know these people over the years. But many of them are frustrated with me because it can take days for me to return their calls. I could maybe have Sally pick that up. To be honest, I'd miss it. And Sally can be stern sounding.

I hear that she is reluctant to give up the relationship connections, and that Sally's style may make her hesitant to delegate to her.

J: Have you had complaints about that?

F: Not many, but I hear it. Most of the people who work closely know she's helpful. She wants to get the job done. It's just that she can be blunt and direct. With outside people that's not so great. It's the people who know her who give her more latitude about her style.

J: What could you do to alert Sally that you want her to develop a broader range of communication styles?

F: I don't want to criticize or insult her; she's really dependable and responsive. I could point out when I hear her being patient. She does do that. She can give a good status update on something if she doesn't feel to pressured.

J: Anything else?

F: I could role-play a conversation with her. That seems obvious, but I've never done it. We could practice doing that ahead of time on a few of our more challenging client conversations.

She has a lot of Action readily in mind.

J: What do you think of these steps?

F: They're good. I just needed to think it through out loud, instead of being always on autopilot, slogging through my list, thinking I can't slow down enough to have others help me.

I'm Thinking she needs to zoom back out to her motivation to take these new Actions.

J: What will help you to remember to try these new steps?

F: Not fighting with my husband. And the sound of the cello. I'll play a recording of one of my favorites on my commute home tonight.

We're just at the beginning of exploring options to help Florence reach her goals of making more personal time by delegating. We are also making progress toward her manager's goal of enjoying her work. Florence is Action-oriented, so her plan to take new steps plays to her strengths.

Steven—Managing Managers

Steven was the software manager of a team within a financial services organization. He had been promoted a few months earlier, and with that the team had grown from four to a dozen. Now he was managing managers, too. We had just met with his manager, Doreen, regarding development goals for our coaching engagement.

J (Janet): What do you think about Doreen's goals for your role and our coaching together?

S (Steven): I really agree that I'm in new territory here. I'm at the awkward haircut stage regarding my staff— you know, when you feel like your hair is too long to look good, but not so long it's time for a haircut. There are too many staff for me to effectively manage, but not enough to justify an assistant manager.

J: How would you describe your team?

S: We have a culture of collective ADD, Attention Deficit Disorder. We do a lot of things at once. Can't focus. We get interested in random projects. React to curious inquiries. Where do you think I should begin to be coached?

That's a quick zoom in on his part. I don't Think we've adequately explored the context and bigger picture. I want my clients to drive the pace and direction of our coaching.

J: Let me not answer that yet. Let's start with your assessment. What is most on your mind? What makes you lose sleep?

S: George. He's a good worker. I've worked with him the longest, maybe seven years. He's competent and respected among his peers. Day-to-day I don't really know what he does. I can't tell how productive he is. And I think at this point he should be taking on some management, such as mentoring others and supervising their work. He likes to do things on his own. I don't know if I should keep him if he won't take on more.

J: I'm hearing a value of up or out—that he should take on management responsibilities or leave. Is that what you're thinking?

S: *(Evading the question)* It's because he told us he wanted something new, but when we offered him a new role, he didn't take it. I don't know why. Maybe he didn't like that manager or that group where he would have been working.

I hear that George is a concern, partly because Steven is not clear on George's motivations. And partly because Steven may have expectations about wanting George to take on more. I need to zoom in on his concerns and what he is Thinking.

J: So you're not clear on his ambitions, his career goals?

S: Right.

J: And it sounds like you're not sure he's pulling his weight?

S: I just don't know.

J: Is there anything else regarding George's not taking on some management responsibilities? Is there anything about your own management load that may apply here?

Here I'm zooming from George back to Steven.

S: Yes. That's true. I do feel overloaded in the management arena, because I still have a lot of my own work to do. I also have to figure out if the team's workloads are fair and helping them grow.

Now it sounds to me like he's overwhelmed at the size of the task, so I want to see if he can view it in a more manageable way. Let's zoom back in, to an Action.

J: What is one thing you can do that is top of your mind in order to get a better sense of what your department needs?

S: I'm in a quandary. I'm increasingly distanced from each member of my group. Should I be? Now I'm managing managers. I've been thinking I want to define one thing—one growth area that each of them needs to develop that would have the biggest impact.

J: That sounds productive, and it sounds like you're clear that would be a good use of your time. Choosing one skill for each one to develop. What else is on your mind?

S: My manager, Doreen, is supportive, generally, but she doesn't think that everyone in my group has a clear plan of what they're working on. They don't keep me informed on milestones. I'm not always clear about where things stand when she asks about the different projects. She doesn't want to see them flailing. That's the word she uses. I don't want my management style to be characterized that way—as flailing.

What he is describing might be a communication issue— or it might be a productivity issue. Doreen is zoomed out to the overall impression, but may not have given Steven good information about the data she is using. Is it just that she doesn't know, or is it that she doesn't have confidence that Steven even knows what is going on and is monitoring and ensuring progress? I want Steven to zoom in on Doreen's point of view, shine the light through into those eyes.

J: Why might she describe your department as flailing?

S: I think it's because I can't always give a status update when she's in meetings with her managers. It's complicated. We are matrixed, and everyone has multiple projects with multiple stakeholders. People from other departments will make a request of one of my folks. I don't want to get bureaucratic and say they can't do that. That's not our culture.

Time to zoom in on what he is Thinking—as well as what he believes Doreen is Thinking.

J: Has she indicated what would have her be more comfortable?

S: She suggested that I assign a "godfather" to each project. Three of my staff are managing small teams, and then there are projects that cross teams. I think it's a good idea.

Good to know Doreen has a request and that Steven supports it. Now I'm zooming back in to Doreen's perspective.

J: What specifically do you think you should do in the next few weeks to meet your manager's request and begin to change the impression she has of your group?

S: I'm going to establish one-on-one meetings with my managers, as well as a monthly meeting with the entire team. That will let me be more informed, and help establish priorities. Then I need to be more disciplined about having regular meetings with Doreen, and come in proactively to give her status updates.

Steven had stepped too far back after delegating, leaving himself open to criticism by his manager. Doreen seemed concerned he didn't have enough knowledge of milestones and outcomes. Sometimes the focus needs to be through someone else's eyes. Well-intentioned managers who appreciate autonomy often will extend too much latitude to their staff. It can leave their staff unclear about expectations, time lines, priorities and deliverables, and upper management concerned about accountability. Connecting with his three managers in one-on-one meetings—and then with the whole group once a month—are good ways to keep informed without holding on too tightly.

Thomas—Accountability

Thomas was well loved by his staff. He was excellent at enrolling them, letting them know what they did well, and delivering corrective feedback, if needed, in a way that motivated them but didn't sting. He enjoyed management and Chuck, his manager, certainly wanted these strengths to continue. However, Chuck needed Thomas to raise the bar on accountability. He was concerned that some of Thomas' people did not deliver on results, and felt they could get away with it. There were small problems with accuracy and a few problems with deliverables. He needed to "strengthen that muscle," so that Chuck could continue to expand Thomas' responsibilities.

J (Janet): What do you think of these goals—do they resonate for you?

T (Thomas): Yes, I'm really glad Chuck has shown this interest in me, and has been direct about where I need to grow. I feel like he wants me to succeed.

J: What about the accountability piece?

T: It's true. I don't always follow up. I don't want to micromanage, and I have built a strong rapport with my staff.

I want to get oriented to the Actions he currently taking.

J: What is it that you do that is so effective with your staff?

T: I meet with them regularly. I believe in management-by-walking around. I show an interest in their personal life because I *am* interested. And I expose them to new opportunities. Whenever I can, I'll bring them to a management or client meeting.

J: What about holding them accountable? What do you currently do?

T: I agree, that's not as strong. I have worked hard to build a strong relationship with each of them, so I tend to put something on the table that needs to be done and see who volunteers. And I do get volunteers. But maybe I'm not always clear about deadlines. I figure they'll use their own good judgment about when they can get to it.

J: And if you were more clear about deadlines?

T: I guess what holds me back is that I treat them as I want to be treated. If Chuck asks me to do something, it goes right on my list and I get to it. I don't want him to ask me every day: How's it going? That would stress me out and feel like mistrust.

Good: Thomas has a clear read on his Feelings, motivations, and reluctance.

J: Is there a time Chuck has checked in and it's felt helpful?

T: Actually, yes, with the X project. It was really big, involved a lot of moving parts, and input from other departments. It was high profile, too, and received a lot of attention from the executives. I had to get cooperation from people who don't work directly for me. So I was glad when Chuck asked about it. There were a few times I needed support. I needed him to raise this project as a priority. He was great.

J: So it didn't feel like micromanaging—or that he mistrusted you?

T: No.

Zooming in to the Actions that were supportive...

J: What was it about the way he did it that helped? That didn't seem intrusive?

T: Hmn, I think that I knew he had my back. I recognized that his questions were really about helping me create the best result, and were not about checking up on me. I knew he wanted me to look good, and for the project to succeed.

J: Anything else?

I'm still shining the light on Actions that Chuck took that were not offensive to Thomas. Those Actions that created positive Feelings.

T: His offers to help were genuine. And, if I got stuck, he let me think out loud with him without me worrying that he would take it over or think I couldn't handle it.

J: Okay so if you summarized those things...what could you try with your staff to maintain the strong relationships and be supportive, yet stay closer to their progress?

T: Check in more regularly. I could make a point to do that casually, asking about progress. I know who is really focused and who on my team tends to get more distracted. So I can use that to decide how often to ask. I can make sure that my questions sound genuinely curious and not critical or skeptical. And offer to just think out loud with them, if they reach a dilemma or a hurdle.

J: How does that strike you, taking those Actions?

T: Good, I can try all that.

It will be a change in habit for him. I wonder which way of Thinking will support that.

J: What would make this worthwhile, this new way of holding people accountable?

T: Remembering that I always wanted good results from my team. I guess I just wasn't as clear and consistent with the follow-up. But remembering that this approach, of showing interest, isn't completely new can be helpful. And then I can think about how Chuck does it works for me. I suppose the fact that my boss wants this change is a motivator!

Taking new Actions can be iterative. Try something, see if it Feels authentic, see if it works, then tweak it. Motivation matters. Habits are there for a reason; they provide efficiency, so clear motivation can support taking some chances on changes. This takes time and effort. Being aware that he appreciates the experience of his manager checking in gives him a visceral experience of a positive form of follow-up. This is different from the concern he had: his anticipation that holding people accountable may cause a negative reaction. Instead he felt supported, and that reframing of the issue may lower the barrier to more frequent follow-up as well.

Frank—Inviting Inquiry

Frank was in line for promotion. He had been told by his boss that he had an amazing track record for creating results. Frank knew that and was proud of it. His boss, Peter, wanted to groom him for the next level of leadership. Peter knew that part of Frank's impressive results were due to being stubborn and driven. He could be a bit of a bull in a china shop. He could steamroll other people. The interviews with peers and staff revealed that he tended to discourage questions or recommendations. Peter also knew that a different approach was learnable. Frank just needed to develop new ways of interacting; he already brought expertise and motivation to the table.

J (Janet): What is most pressing for you right now?

F (Frank): I don't really know the metrics of success for my pending promotion. How will I know I've succeeded?

Peter has said I am allowed to define that to a certain extent, around the edges. The areas where I'm really struggling are where boundaries are not well defined.

J: It sounds like a lot of uncertainty.

F: The technical challenge is easier, in a way. Even though we're in a whole new area, I know how to approach problem-solving. I'm confident about that. But with this uncertainty, my moods cycle during the week.

I could explore the Feeling of moodiness, but I decide to hone in on the cause of it.

J: What else do you know about your relationship with uncertainty?

F: It's easy to get lost in the weeds of daily requests. I like the hands-on part; I like to *do* some of the work. I like action. It's easy to let that take more time than it should. So I tend to keep doing that. It keeps uncertainty away.

The light is shining on his taking Action. Is there anything he's avoiding? I also want to be sure we come back to his uncertainty.

J: What gets left undone?

F: It's less comfortable to engage people. It's harder with the group than one-on-one. I feel more effective when the other person who works for me drives and I steer a little. I like when they ask questions—except often they don't—and that may be what Peter is after. Maybe there's something I'm doing that prevents them from asking questions or suggesting improvements.

If the Action he wants to focus on is the thing he's avoiding—engaging his staff—then this is where I need to zoom in. Let's look at Act.

J: What might you be doing that prevents them from asking questions?

F: I do know a lot more technically than my staff—so I tend to blurt out which direction we should go in. I don't want to hold back just for the entertainment—what's the point of that? Why would I hold back when I have information that could help?

There's another choice as a manager besides insisting on a direction or withholding information. We'll explore that. First, I want to shine a light on his confidence.

J: What do you know about your confidence?

F: In the workshop you gave you mentioned people's orientation to confidence, motivation, and feedback. Rather than "internal locus of control" vs. "external locus of control," I like to think of it as a gyroscope or radar. They are both useful tools. Both tools do something practical. I'm more radar. I trained as a physicist, so this metaphor makes sense for me. I'm always scanning the environment. I'm aware of what else is going on around me. It gives me confidence. I can remember multiple projects, I can see industry trends, and I can scan for political hot buttons—if I remember to. Maybe it's something that Peter values, my strategic view.

J: Great. What about the gyroscope?

F: Those are the people who orient internally; they can be confident too, but it's a different point of view. It's their ability to right themselves, metaphorically; it's a confidence that's inward facing. Like a cat landing on all four feet, no matter what height it falls from.

It sounds like he has a good grasp of alternative perspectives, but I don't know much about gyroscopes or radar systems, so I probe further to help understand his metaphor.

J: How does that affect how you manage?

F: I want more time to develop people. I want to foster knowledge sharing. I don't think that's Peter's vision for my group.

J: If you were to spend more time with your team despite Peter's thinking it's not a priority, do you believe you will still land on your feet?

F: Yes. I want to be sure to meet his expectations yet also be the kind of manager I want to be.

J: Is that a question?

F: The reporting relationships are vague and flexible, as is my group's mission—and our boundaries. Where does my group's job end and others begin? I think Peter shares the view that it's vague and unclear, but I'm not sure.

Here he is zoomed out to the difficulties of organization structure and accountabilities. He's already told me he's good at radar—taking in the environment. I want to zoom in to the Actions he can take, to help him land on his feet.

J: Given that Peter has given you some latitude, what are some actions you can take or propose to take?

F: I want to cross train my team. They are too isolated from each other and can't really cover for each other. That would be development for them. And giving them some visibility at management meetings they don't normally attend. I also want to create a training program for new hire researchers, so they can use our computerized lab systems more independently.

J: Great, what would be next steps?

F: I think I would begin both of those on a small scale, develop some traction, and then report back to Peter. I'd let him know what I've tried and what has worked. Then I'd get input from him. He does have a more political perspective, which can be valuable

Once Frank brought his focus to next steps, he was quite clear about the approaches he had in mind. Taking Action seemed to reduce his Feelings of uncertainty. An incremental approach to development and training can work well with his manager. Often managers such as Peter want to be included but not be responsible for improvements, so planning and beginning implementation is often an effective way to present a new approach.

Taking Action is as natural as breathing; it is what produces results. In fact, it is so natural that Action can be taken without first reflecting upon or anticipating impact. It is hard to slow down when the to-do list is long and imposing. Yet sometimes Actions are busy work, not the most leveraged, bang for the buck, or strategic.

Nora was faced with a fairly common challenge: having to protect her staff from her manager. She was somewhat stymied by the dilemma, which called for her to be true to her own judgment *and* be responsive to her manager's concerns. She did have control over helping her employee (Roger) see the benefits of modifying his behavior. By guiding Roger to broaden his focus on treating managers like customers, he could apply his usual Actions (good customer service) in a new arena.

As Lee considered the rate of change at her company, she struggled to hold on to her areas of expertise and share what she knows while retaining accountability for the final results. She realized she could influence the design of her morphing role, which offered some sense of control—even in uncertainty.

Florence was so used to working hard, Acting, that her boss wanted her to change that. It was a long standing habit, which required a refocus. Working harder sometimes crowds out working smarter. Giving herself time to reflect, she realized it was something she wanted, too.

Managing managers is a special challenge, which requires a new way of thinking. Steven needed to evolve his old delegating habit to be more specific, and provide more monitoring. This change in Action requires a change in Thinking; now he needs to focus on keeping track without interfering or micromanaging. Based on his positive experience of having his manager follow-up, he realized he could stay closer to projects in a way that motivated.

Frank was comfortable with the technology—being "in the weeds" as he called it—and less comfortable with the more unpredictable aspects of relationship building. It's messier! As a result, his own staff found him unapproachable—an outcome he did not want. In fact, as he described his own management goals, they included developing others. This gave him greater impetus to Act in a way that was congruent with that goal.

4

LENS THREE—FEEL

The concept of Feeling is gaining greater respect in the workplace. "In the business world, we are taught to approach organizational challenges objectively and logically," Carol Ginsey Goman wrote. "We quantify everything we can and guard against emotions that would hijack our objectivity..... Brain science makes it clear that...logical reasoning is often no more than a way to justify emotional choices."

The mind/body connection, for example, highlights the importance of thought on Feelings: the things you Think about affect how you Feel. Mindfulness opens the awareness that thoughts are optional. We can decide what we Think about, rather than be subject to the tidal wave of random thoughts. Mindfulness of Thinking and Feeling has a positive impact on health and well-being. Many clients have reaped the benefits of mindfulness practices, which are gaining greater respect in the workplace due to its benefits on emotional health. These may include regular practices of meditation, journaling, reflection, or a walk in nature.

Google employee Chade-Meng Tan wrote a wonderful book about mindfulness, which was appropriately titled for a search engine employee: *Search Inside Yourself*. The book was cowritten with Daniel Goleman, the author of the groundbreaking *Emotional Intelligence*, who first consolidated research demonstrating that emotions are more important for success than IQ. Chade-Meng Tan presented mindfulness ideas to many Google engineers, who may have been skeptical or reluctant at first, but some were convinced of its benefits. There is a connection between mindfulness and Feeling, because it is in that state that we are most able to sense nuanced feelings. Being mindful when feelings and their related sensations are beginning—rather than waiting until they are pounding on the door of our consciousness—has great advantages over letting Feelings simmer and be disregarded and denied. This approach, which one of my colleagues calls "stack attack," ignoring and stacking up feelings inside, can result in annoyances getting pent up and then exploding at some unexpected, inopportune time.

Happiness research (such as in *Happiness Advantage*, by Shawn Achor, among others) provides tips and strategies for maintaining happiness, demonstrating that the Feeling of happiness actually precedes goal attainment and is the precursor to productivity. This is not to say that all Feelings are happy or that happiness is always the goal. Rather, I would argue that the goal is awareness. Feelings have valuable information that can inform Actions and decisions.

Some leaders are reluctant to access Feelings, although they are a legitimate source of valuable information. Their reluctance may come from their experience that uncomfortable Feelings may lead to unedited Actions. Expressing impatience or anger may momentarily release tension. The subsequent result may be an unfortunate impact. However, awareness of Feelings serves as data to inform options and Actions; they have the potential to become the hallmark of a developing leader.

AJ's Missed Targets

AJ had been working for a software company for several years, and came to his organization with previous experience in general management. He had been Feeling a lot of pressure as of late because he had missed some performance targets. His manager, Don, sometimes played bad cop, criticizing AJ and coming down hard on him. At other times, Don seemed supportive of AJ and blamed the next level manager, Andrew for the pressure. By several measures AJ had a good year, but agreed with Don that he hadn't achieved the key performance indicators by fiscal year end. In a meeting with Don the day before, he was only focused on the missed targets despite all of the other contributions during the year, and AJ was fuming.

> AJ: I had the meeting with Don. He wants to reduce my base, not just my bonus, based on not meeting targets.

> J (Janet): Oh?

> AJ: I can't believe that. What kind of message is that to send?

> J: What's the worst part of that for you?

> AJ: (Irritated.) Don isn't taking into account all the work we've done in our division laying the groundwork, delivering to our existing customers, improving processes, and building staff. I know you're pleased that I'm not angry.

> *Since I have not given him this advice I'm Thinking this is a red flag. Too often people zoom out from their Feelings, which reduces valuable information. Feelings drive Actions and reactions and point to important values. I wanted to have him zoom back in.*

J: No, I think emotions carry important information. I don't have a recommendation that says you shouldn't be angry.

AJ: Well, maybe I should say I'm not acting out my anger.

J: That's a good plan for your reputation and career. But let's still explore the anger and discover how it can inform you.

AJ: *(Animated.)* They blow off the foundational work I've been doing. They don't realize what it takes to be operating in new regions and multiple states. I successfully set up new distribution networks. They don't appreciate how the process improvements will pay off. It's true I didn't meet some performance goals. I accept it and take responsibility for it.

J: Let's find out more about the anger.

AJ: I didn't meet the profit targets—but they were so arbitrary. Also, Don passes the buck. One minute he's bad cop, slamming me for a missed opportunity or some kind of oversight, the next minute he tries to be good cop and blames *his* manager, Andrew, for the pressure on us. Well, where does *he* stand? How am I supposed to navigate that?

Zooming in again; this isn't just about what's happening, it's about what matters, how he Feels.

J: What's the worst part about that?

AJ: They're playing games. It's just a game—and I'm losing. I'm angry. The rules aren't fair.

J: What else?

AJ: He insisted on adding the new territory even though *I* knew we were not prepared to support the product. Now he's punishing me. Don expects me to make a compelling argument for what happened. That's ridiculous. He's not even going to listen.

I'm recalling that AJ had previously spoken about the relationship between Don and his boss, Andrew. They seemed pretty aligned, including being willing to disagree and argue. But they weren't always clear about where the argument ended and what decision was reached. I'm thinking AJ is zoomed in on the unfairness, which is understandable, but it's making him stuck. Is he ready to zoom out?

J: Let's imagine that Don and Andrew make complete sense, and that you are a cultural anthropologist: someone who studies habits, rituals, artifacts, and even food to understand what is meaningful in a culture. What do you know about their culture?

AJ: When they meet, they always meet over breakfast at 7:00 AM. They kind of blurt out what's on their minds without a lot of careful reflection. They've come up with some big wins, and feel pretty good about how they work together. They've got a long history. I think their arguments are part of the fun for them—part of the energy.

J: What else about their culture?

AJ: They're being stupid.

We're losing the anthropologist metaphor, which is why it's important to acknowledge and understand the emotions. Otherwise emotions trump curiosity, which limits options.

J: What is stupid?

AJ: What's stupid is they aren't taking into account what I've done.

J: Your contributions aren't being acknowledged?

AJ: Right, that's why I'm angry. They don't see what I've done.

J: They don't share your perspective.

AJ: Right!

J: Not being appreciated for your contributions is an understandable source of anger. Are you ready to talk about a new approach?

Let's zoom in to how Don and Andrew aren't sharing his perspective.

AJ: Okay. Maybe.

J: Your perspective is that you've added a lot of value, but that it's not reflected in the metrics they're focusing on.

AJ: Yes, those metrics are selective. And they don't acknowledge the qualitative contributions and long-range groundwork I'm laying.

J: And you...what about you. Do you see their perspective?

By this time I felt I had a good enough rapport with AJ that I could tease him about not being able to explore Don and Andrew's perspective—the exact complaint he had about them. So let's shine the light on their perspective.

AJ: *(Laughing)*. I'm mad they can't see my perspective. But if they made sense—and they don't—it might be because they built their goals on top of my goals, which they made up, and my goals weren't met.

Sometimes the spotlight moves without needing to get closer or further. It merely pans the landscape settling on a new target and that, in of itself, brings a new perspective and fresh options.

In his next session, AJ reported that he was able to gain more distance from the feeling of injustice and recognize that his boss had disappointments related to AJ's own results. AJ was able to reclaim his ability to stay focused on what he was accomplishing and gain some peace. At the same time, he resolved to have a more open dialogue about obstacles and more conversations about contingencies. If he found himself unable to achieve performance indicators because the organization had shifted focus midstream, he would be more direct about renegotiating expectations. Or he would conclude that it wasn't the right place for him any longer.

Pat—Reducing Defensiveness

Pat was a software director who was knowledgeable and seemingly confident, yet her defensiveness, which she acknowledged, was holding her back. Her manager, Mark, had identified Pat's technical and project management strengths and, for the most part, was able to focus the role on them.

There was a recent incident however, in which Pat had released a product update without sufficient testing, and it proved disastrous. Mark confronted Pat about it and said she would be marginalized and at-risk career wise if she didn't adhere to procedures and gain buy-in from the broader group. She was quite defensive and didn't take responsibility for the disaster. Mark was direct, reminding her this is not the kind of culture where she can act like a star or a cowboy. After she had a few days to digest the feedback, she thanked Mark.

She said no one had ever given her feedback like that, and she realized she has to be more careful with procedures, communication, and enrolling others.

"She was quite gracious about it," Mark said. "I'm sure it was hard to hear. There is such a thing as good self-promotion, but Pat was demonstrating the insecure kind. If you need all the credit, this place won't be a fit. I am hoping she will continue to develop her newfound awareness."

J (Janet): What would you like to work on today?

P (Pat): I know defensiveness is an issue. I guess I'm a fighter. I've always been told I'm smart, and I've had regular promotions. All of that has reinforced my position that I have a lot to offer.

J: Mark agrees with that.

It's important early in a coaching relationship to remind leaders that we'll be working from strengths. I'm listening for her awareness of the Feeling of defensiveness.

P: I've identified defensiveness as my top priority.

J: Let's explore that a little. What do you know about that?

P: I've been in environments that were much more competitive than this, where you had to stand firm to get any support for a project. It was in the culture there, so I didn't stick out. Being aggressive was necessary. In my old company I don't even think it was considered defensiveness.

I'm curious about the Feeling of defensiveness, and how awareness of that may free her a little. I'm going to zoom in there.

J: What do you know about that reaction in yourself—outside of your last company?

P: I feel that someone questioning my ideas is a personal attack. It *does* make me defensive. My ideas are my contribution—they are *me*, so I feel like I have to stand up for myself.

To explore her goal of reducing her defensiveness, I want to zoom out from that Thought—that someone challenging her ideas is perceived by her as a personal attack.

J: If you distance yourself from the notion that when people question you about your ideas it's a personal attack, what do you notice?

P: I have to think about that.

J: Let's take a situation that occurred a month or so ago. How you feel about it today?

P: (Thinks for a while.) Joel recently commented on my designs. I remember the familiar feeling of defensiveness, and he also proposed an improvement that turned out to be helpful.

J: As you look back on that, what do you notice about your Feelings?

P: I'm not aggravated or defensive.

J: So when the challenge includes the recommendation this changes your reactions?

P: I feel more constructive. I know I'm open-minded. I don't want to be seen as defensive. I really want to be a better manager and encourage conversations. It's really about how I manage relationships with people.

Today I was aware of doing that. Someone wanted to change the specifications of some things my group is working on. Changing something we're already doing is a huge pain. But I slowed down and remembered to ask more about it. I was more focused on the inquiry. I realized I didn't feel frustrated.

J: What did you notice about that?

P: I put myself in their shoes. I thought about what they were trying to accomplish. It happens the other person is someone I like who is reasonable, which made it easier.

She had zoomed more into Feeling—and even into what the other person was Feeling.

J: What enabled you to do that?

P: It's just becoming easier. In software development there's an expression, "agile methodology": If you just name it and watch it, it changes. I feel like that about defensiveness. It's changed just by my being more aware of it. Talking about it can surface a solution.

J: That sounds like a successful approach.

P: I just shifted the conversation a little. I'm being more patient and asking more questions. It makes a real difference. Phrase things differently and check what they're looking for. I can modulate my message if I'm thinking it's a bad idea, or they may even change my decision. I'm being more aware—more deliberate to highlight their point and let them know where I agree.

J: What enabled you to do that?

I want to zoom in and harvest the awareness she has had. Her software expertise provided her with a terrific metaphor. The Feelings of defensiveness can be rooted to any number of causes. That awareness can continue to bolster her commitment to this change.

P: Remembering the way I'm being seen and knowing I want that to change. I'm going to keep those things in mind: I want to be seen not just as an expert, but also as a constructive colleague.

Pat was being asked to examine her defensiveness and craft a different way of responding when she felt criticized or obstructed. As we talked through this challenge, she had an insight that her profession of software development provided her with a metaphor that deeply resonated to her. Agile development, an iterative and developmental approach to software, could be used to modify her defensive reaction to challenges and afford the opportunity to try small steps, get feedback, and modify again.

Connie—Inner Bully

In previous sessions, Connie had talked about how she could second guess herself and worry a lot about whether she was doing a good job. She was a fairly young manager, and still getting her bearings in her new big role. Because her anecdotes did not include any data about complaints or criticism, we had referred to these worries as her "inner bully." She said the label helped her, as she was able to separate the inner bully entity from herself.

J (Janet): So what would you like to cover today, Connie?

C (Connie): The calming techniques you gave me last time are working, but I keep checking with others to make sure my reports are sufficient even though I'm actually pretty confident with my recommendations and presentations.

J: How often is your data right?

C: Usually. But when I'm asked a question that feels challenging I freeze up, even when I know the answer. I hate that.

J: Can you give me an example?

Zooming in to the circumstances that are causing the uncomfortable Feeling.

C: Recently, in a presentation, I used data provided by my boss, Greg, and built on that. When I was challenged about the data, I got flustered. I felt put on the spot. I wasn't going to blame Greg in the meeting. But I wasn't careless—I didn't do it wrong—maybe I just overly relied on his information. Then I started yelling at myself inside, and couldn't really come up with a response. I froze.

I'm Thinking we need to zoom into the inner bully, which is causing these Feelings. What was the inner bully trying to do for her? The focus was deeply on self-criticism. Her inner critic wasn't really helping her out right now, but what were its best intentions?

J: What do you think your inner bully might be trying to do for you?

C: To protect me against judgment from others. It's also guarding me against my fear of being perceived as unintelligent, as unworthy of being part of the team.

J: Connie, did you know this issue of self-doubt is so prevalent it even has a name? *Impostor syndrome.* Being afraid others will see you as an impostor -as not being worthy of the role you're in.

C: *(Relieved.)* Really?

J: Yes—even accomplished senior level executives experience this.

C: It helps to know that. But I still feel like an impostor. I feel anxious, especially in meetings.

I'm thinking it is time to zoom into her Feelings.

J: What happens then?

C: Feeling anxious makes me more apprehensive. I become less articulate, which causes my boss to tell me to "be more confident." This makes me more anxious.

It was time to have her zoom out from Feeling anxious and move the spotlight to finding a role she could embody. I was looking for us to shine a light on other possibilities.

J: Imagine that in meetings you were a UN Representative, an Ambassador to a foreign country, or a hostess of a gathering. It was your role to put everyone else at ease. What image comes to mind?

C: (Pause.) Greeters in Hawaii. When you visit, greeters appear when the plane arrives and hand out those colorful real flower necklaces, leis.

J: Great. At the next meeting you attend—even if it's not your meeting—bring to mind that image. Make it your responsibility to put everyone else at ease. Imagine the feeling of being a greeter, smiling and being glad to see everyone. In your mind's eye you are handing out flower leis.

C: I like that. There's one more thing. I feel like everyone here is on a different page—that I don't really get the culture or share the company's values. I'm not ready to quit because I want to make this work.

I'm hearing that she's too focused on the differences and not feeling resourceful. Zooming out from the discomfort, I suggest that she change the focus from shining the light on differences to spotlighting her learning.

J: Imagine that this job is a graduate-level program. That you to attend this graduate program for free, and you will even be paid. Your task is to understand other people's behavior and values—even when they are different from yours.

C: Okay, I can do that.

There were two elements we were working on. One was her anxiety in meetings, where she was zoomed in on her anxiety about whether her data was correct. Since it usually was, that wasn't much review or rework that was needed. If she had reported that she made lots of errors that would have suggested a different approach. But her anxiety largely came from within. It's not enough to say to someone "don't feel anxious" or "be more confident." It's not even respectful. But by reframing the situation and giving her a different role in her mind as a greeter, she could alter her perspective.

The second element was feeling out of the norm. She had not provided any convincing data or examples indicating others regarded her this way, though that is still possible. In the meantime, since she was an avid learner she was able to resonate with the idea of studying her co-workers. For our next session, we would further explore whether zooming out of Feeling like she doesn't belong and researching the facts and feelings about the culture can provide new perspective.

Pedro—Informed by His Feelings

I've worked with Pedro, who manages a large team of nurses, on and off for years; generally we have sessions when he gets a promotion. He has become attuned to his own reactions, especially when something isn't quite right. He calls it "feeling off."

P (Pedro): I know something is bothering me when I "feel off." I've been feeling off about Arlene. She's been here for six years, and I know what she's able to do. I know she was disappointed that she didn't get promoted from Supervisor to Manager. I've been mulling that over, noticing I'm unsettled, bothered..."feeling off."

Although he has not yet named the Feeling, he's making it clear where to zoom in.

J (Janet): Let's explore that a little more and get closer to that feeling. What are you noticing?

P: I think what I'm struggling with is her desire to get a promotion. I know she's smart, capable, and has advanced degrees. She was hurt that I hired someone in over her—not really over her, but more senior. Arlene still reports to me, not the new person—but she still saw that as a big disappointment or maybe even betrayal.

J: What in particular about that is troubling you?

P: I'm distracted, wishing it would go away. I'm exhausted knowing I need to deal with it. I'm frustrated that she says one thing and does another. I'm feeling really mixed.

He has effectively zoomed in to discover more about his combination of Feelings.

J: You have a lot of awareness of why you're feeling off.

P: She says she wants the promotion, but I've been clear about what I've asked her for. I worry. I guess it's my fault I haven't followed up as much as I should. I've asked her for this report and that process—and then I'll remember a month later that I haven't received either of them.

I want to zoom into that feeling of worry.

J: Let's look a little deeper to see what you feel when you think about not having followed up. It sounds like you may be worrying that you own some part of this.

P: I know I haven't always kept track of her progress or even been explicit about due dates. But she's a senior staff member—should I really have to? Can't I just say what I want and it will get done?

J: Hmm.

P: She does the things she's good at—what she likes and has always done. Then she says she wants more responsibility, but doesn't take it on when I offer it. So I don't feel I have enough evidence to show she can handle more.

J: You feel she may not be willing to do what it takes to manage the next level role?

P: Right.

Sometimes we have to zoom out to review two competing Feelings or ideas.

J: Tell me if I understand this correctly. On the one hand, you feel that you might share some responsibility for her not being promoted because you haven't been clear about deadlines and priorities. On the other, you feel that she should demonstrate greater commitment and ownership to give you confidence in her ability to handle more responsibility.

P: Yes. She's a hard worker and she's been here a long time. She always goes the extra mile for patients. But she is fighting fires, not managing her team. She likes being the hero in an emergency. I want her to manage her team. She needs to be more strategic. But I don't want to be rude. I don't want to marginalize her work and her successes. She's very dedicated.

J: So you don't want to be rude and you want to acknowledge her contributions, yet it sounds like something is holding you back from expressing that thought. Is that right?

He has zoomed in to one side of the equation. Let's see what the other side is, where else the spotlight needs to shine. I wonder if he can switch between the two Feelings.

P: Yes. I've told her what it takes to be promoted. But when I think about it she isn't even taking on all the aspects of her current role. I've told her it's her job to produce the monthly reports. She still doesn't get to it. I've asked her to follow up with our referring physicians and all she says is she left a message, "What am I supposed to do?" She leaves it at that.

J: When you hear those stories, what matters most to you?

I wonder whether he will zoom in to his Feeling...

P: There's a disconnect between what she says she wants and how she's acting. Also, I can't count on her. I don't want to have to be the one to follow up all the time. I want her to say, "Here are the numbers, I see where there's a problem. This is what I'm going to do to address it. Here's what the staff need to learn—and I've scheduled that." I want her to be pushing me, saying I finished that project now and can take on more from you. Then I worry that's just about me wanting to offload my projects, which is true. I do want to delegate, but am I being fair?

By asking more about his Feelings, we zoom in to his inner experience and the root cause of his inner alarm. He recognizes that sometimes he has to wait through feeling off and for the source of the discontent to reveal itself. No point in zooming out yet; he knows his own process. I do, however, want to find out about his Thinking.

J: You've identified that your feeling off is partly due to the contradiction of her goal of wanting to take on more but her failure to be proactive. Specifically, what do you think would demonstrate the new level of management competence you are looking for her to prove?

This zooms out from his Feelings—which, for the moment, have been identified—and brings him part way to an Action step informed by the root of those Feelings.

P: She needs to meet regularly with her staff about developing their own skills—not just about patient conditions. I'd like to see her create opportunities for them to learn from each other about technique and intuition, not just how they are dealing with certain patients. It's important that the team bonds over something other than feeling wrung out. I think it just drags everyone down. She'll join in on the complaining and whining, and it's one thing her people love about her. But it's not really managerial behavior.

It sounds like he is ready to move into Thinking and designing an Action—both for himself and regarding his approach to Arlene.

J: As an interim step, how might she demonstrate to you that she's moving towards meeting your expectations?

P: She could hold regular meetings with her department, bring issues that she's identified and the resolutions she's implemented, anticipate staffing needs, and learn to report quantitative, as well as qualitative, progress.

Pedro has a well attuned to his alarm system, his own process of dealing with his feelings of unrest. He is willing to explore and be informed by them. Once he was able to raise them into awareness, he could pinpoint next steps.

Raphael—Tames His Inner Bulldog

Raphael is an engineer in a consulting company, and he's very good in his niche. In fact, he's so skilled that he's argumentative if someone else has an idea that is different from his. Clients love him, however, because he's tenacious and innovative in his approach, grappling with regulators and bureaucrats in a way that gets the job done. But he's not working well with his own partners. He agrees he's creating tension and difficulties inside the company and doesn't like the impact; he Feels that he's not getting the credit he deserves for creating good client relationships. He becomes combative when convinced that his approach is the right one. He says that his tenaciousness makes him seem like a "bulldog" to others. But Raphael is willing to discover different approaches so that he can project a willingness to listen to alternative problem-solving approaches while still achieving the same results. In the scenario below, he informs me about a specific confrontation with George, his colleague.

J (Janet): Where would you like to start today?

R (Raphael): You heard about the blow up with George. I feel comfortable with him, so I let loose when I became excited and aggravated over our disagreement. It aggravated me that we didn't understand each other. I know it's important for me *not* to get excited like that. It's like when my sister and I would fight. I shouldn't be that familiar with George. In fact, I didn't even like when it happened with my sister. I shouldn't have gotten so pushy.

I'm hearing that he already wants to put this behind him, but there may be more to discover by zooming in to this Feeling.

J: What was it that made you feel so strongly?

R: I had a really good approach. I knew it was innovative and creative. George said it was crazy. I don't know, I feel like he started it—but that's not the point.

J: So you felt pleased about your idea?

R: Yeah, that was the feeling. I really wanted to go with it 'cause it was great. I get that it's my own stubbornness that's in the way of good debate.

J: Is that your intention—to create a debate?

R: Yes, but in the "may the best man win" kind of way. We'd debate so I could prove my point. Get him to see.

J: When did you notice the conversation was getting off track?

R: George was turning red, and I could hear myself interrupting him. I have this need to act like I'm the smartest guy in the room. I have to listen to this feedback because my wife says I do that at home, too. I flaunt that I'm the cleverest. I'm not trying to do that. I realize that I'm seen as pontificating, and I don't want to keep doing that.

Although he hasn't named them, I'm hearing several potential Feelings. I'm hearing that he feels confident, maybe an awareness of some regret, and perhaps some embarrassment about his own behavior. I wonder if Raphael Feels he would be giving up some identity by altering his approach. As an intellectual, he prefers the Thinking lens, whereas others are reacting to him through their Feeling lens.

J: What might motivate you to try out something different?

R: Sometimes I just want to say, "This is me, this is who I am. Deal with it." The short answer is, all of what I do is fine. I know how to build rapport with 80% of people.

Still needing to zoom in on his Feelings...

J: It sounds like you may be a little resentful of these demands to respond differently.

R: I am resentful, but I realize I could learn how to deliver my ideas differently.

J: You're building that muscle. You know how to solve problems and be inventive. Keep all that. Just add curiosity and rapport. Nobody complained about your ability, competence, or intelligence. You are effective with a large percentage of people you deal with, including clients.

R: Staff do like me. I play softball, I bring them chocolates. Just last week a client recommended me to a new client in front of the senior partners. But still so much criticism. I feel like I'm on the Apollo 13 and I'm running out of oxygen.

Time to move the spotlight from Feeling and shine in on Action.

J: So when you think of buying time, letting your partners see that you are committed to making a change, and rechanneling your bulldog approach, what do you want to try?

R: For starters, I could talk less. I know I take up more than my share of time at meetings and that my enthusiasm causes me to talk over others. Some people know that's just being dynamic and involved, but I can see that I leave others in the dust. They think of it as grandstanding. I know because one of my friends in the company told me that. In fact, this reminds me—I once dated a girl who was really nice. We were together for years, but she was from a quiet, polite family who didn't fight, and I'm from a family who always had arguments at the dinner table. We weren't angry with each other, we were just thinking out loud, finding out different points of view, pressing for why ours was the best and theirs was faulty. But my girlfriend and I broke up, because she felt assaulted when I got into that mode—which was regularly.

J: So in a way, you're giving something up. What would make tamping down your expressiveness worth it?

R: Yes, part of me believes that I shouldn't have to keep proving myself. My work should speak for itself. Couldn't they just say, "You get nine out of ten things right" in my job? But I know I'll be a better person if I fix this.

I hear his ambivalence: resentment on the one hand; and a willingness to consider new approaches on the other. Coming back to Act—let's explore his willingness to Act differently.

J: So what's one small concrete thing you want to plan to do differently?

R: I know I have to go meet with George one-on-one. It's a little awkward because once I finish talking—even if I do remember to stop—he'll look out the window as if he's waiting for me to challenge him. But I think it just takes him that long to decide what he wants to say. He doesn't really challenge in the same way I do.

Zooming in a little closer to Act.

J: And then what?

R: Being a better listener would go a long way. George is a pretty fair person, and I'm pretty likable. So I think just really concentrating on listening—making sure I understand his point. Even if I just say it back to him, it will start to move the ship. It's challenging for me. Being this deliberate feels like learning how to ride a bike.

J: Excellent! You know what they say about learning to ride—you never forget.

Raphael felt ambivalent about change. Like all of us, he wanted to be accepted and appreciated just the way he is. He had been extremely successful with a tenacious, expressive approach. He felt resentment that he had to change because others viewed his behavior as argumentative. From his point of view, he was demonstrating energy and vitality, not aggressiveness. Yet he reluctantly agreed he didn't like the fallout of the impact of that behavior, and it was this awareness that motivated him to change.

Ron—Adrenaline Rush

Ron worked in accounting for a large nonprofit. He was responsible for a complicated set of accounting books with all different fiscal year ends and varied tax filing deadlines. He was struggling with some staff issues in his department. His overall goals were to get more credit for all the hard work he and his group contribute. This meant he was also struggling with his ability to influence up.

> R (Ron); Everyone is frustrated. Wally, my boss, is a jerk. When he does reviews he trashes the company. I've got my share of complaints, but this isn't a bad place to work. I like it here. I don't want to have to listen to that. Everybody is stressed out because it's review time. I'm getting pressure because Jack is under scrutiny. Jack works for me, and I think he's proficient. He's as good as anyone. But Wally criticizes Jack, thinks he's lazy. Jack was recently promoted, though. I'm not sure I know what motivates him. I'm frustrated with him too, frankly. He's not paying attention to his new hires. He doesn't get it that you need to spend time with them. He's shown no real initiative to take charge. He hasn't held a department meeting and isn't giving them a good orientation to our department's work. He mystifies me. One minute he does great work; the next, he's laconic. The feedback from an internal customer is that "he does nothing to make my job easier." Another person said, "He doesn't grasp that he's in a support role." That's pretty bad. It kind of reflects on me, too. Wally emphasizes that we're in a support role. Jack hasn't done anything wrong, he's just not take-charge. Not showing initiative. The things he's done are good, but some people complain he hasn't done very much. I have a dossier of information that he is not delivering service. I'm in a quandary. He's a good individual contributor, but not a team player. He says he wants

more money, a higher role, but he's not demonstrating that level of responsibility. I'm puzzled. I'm baffled. I'm angry.

Sometimes you can tell someone is in the Feel lens just by the length of their opening comments.

J (Janet): That's a lot.

R: Okay, I'm done. No, I'm not. Debbie quit. I was going to cancel our meeting because now I feel even more under pressure.

He was zoomed in on a wide range of Feelings due to a deluge of facts. To gain some perspective, we could either zoom in on each Feeling or zoom out to his overall outlook.

J: How do you feel?

R: Overwhelmed.

J: What do you know about yourself when you're overwhelmed?

R: I think there's a part of it I like. I like the adrenalin rush. It makes me feel kind of buzzed. Important. Productive.

This was not the response I was expecting. He had sounded frustrated and paralyzed.

J: Is there anything specific you want to work on today?

Maybe focusing on everything is fine for him, maybe the adrenalin rush is worth it, or maybe there is a top priority to explore.

R: Even though there's a part of the pressure that gives me a buzz, the fact is it also feels like chaos. I know the higher-ups are looking at my department and seeing chaos. I don't like that because I know we do good work.

J: Are you worried about their opinion?

R: Yes and no. I'm *not* worried about their opinion of our work because we do good work. But I *am* worried that they might mischaracterize us.

I want to find out more in terms of which Feeling is stronger—his confidence in his results or his concern about his department's reputation.

J: What do you know about *not* being willing to consider the impact to your reputation?

R: I know my job better than management. I certainly know more than Wally, but it's not just him. It's senior leadership that makes comments about people in my group always being out of the office. I know what has to be done every day, and I always meet my commitments.

J: And the worried part?

R: I worry about their judgment. Even if it's wrong, it can color the way they see my group and me.

It sounds like he is ready to explore this Feeling of worry.

J: If you dig into that worry, what do you know?

R: Maybe it's more like resentment. That they're using the wrong yard stick. That I know what needs to be done more than they do. They don't fill out these crazy forms, they don't know the regulations, they don't know the filing requirements for every state.

J: Getting closer to that resentment, what do you care about?

R: Competence. I know I'm competent. And maybe credit. I want acknowledgment for what I do. Or at least trust. Yeah, trust—for me to know that they know that I'm trustworthy.

I want to zoom in to that issue.

J: And right now what are you feeling?

R: Resentment. That they don't leave us alone. As hard as I work, they can't just trust that I'll manage the department. That I'm making sure Jack does his share.

His Feeling of resentment derives from the experience that he isn't being trusted and isn't being given the latitude to manage his department as he sees fit. Let's zoom in on his Feeling and his willingness to find ways to change management's assessment.

J: Tell me, what do you know about their complaints?

R: Responsiveness is one. They just don't know how much we handle and the pressure we're under for regulatory filings. Two is that when my guys work late I give them compensatory time off the next day. If we're here until midnight I don't make them come in at 8:00 AM the next day. If we're here all Sunday, I may look the other way if they take off Monday.

J: And management objects?

R: Yes. I know my guys give a full week's work—just maybe not on a normal schedule.

J: So you feel justified about being a flexible manager in that way?

R: Yes. But I know they would rather that we plan and get the work done during the day and during the week.

J: It sounds like managing the team's schedule the way you do might be costing you.

R: That's what makes me angry. It's not really a big problem. I don't get it. They're wrong to make a big deal out of this. It's petty. Why can't they just back off?

J: I'm hearing that their focus on timeliness and schedules doesn't match your value for flexibility. And yet it's costing you in terms of management's opinion.

R: Yeah, well, the choice is kind of obvious when you put it that way. I do resent that difference, but maybe they're not wrong. Exactly. Maybe we could just agree to disagree. But since they haven't, maybe I have to agree to agree. It will be challenging to change our work styles. There's something about the marathon push for a deadline that's kind of bonding. You know, pizza and pitching in. But overall, it's not worth the cost if that results in a ding to our reputation.

Ron drew his own conclusion about options: His next step was Action. Once he reflected on his Feelings of resentment—and how management was judging his group—he became clearer about his choices. The main issue was to change the dynamic around his emotions, which were using up his energy and causing him dissatisfaction. There may be other ways to manage up, but Ron had identified next steps. He wasn't happy about the pressure to conform, but realized this was the better option.

Alan—Anger Has a Message

I had been working with Alan for several months. He had significant expertise and knowledge in his regulated industry. His challenge had been to be more responsive, keeping people informed of his progress on projects, and managing his staff to do the same. He described himself as distractible, but justified that as part of his brainstorming process. Letting his mind run free was part of his effective creativity. Being creative *and* compliant with regulations was a challenge and he could walk the line. His boss had previously agreed that Alan was great at that. His staff enjoyed the energy. Even though Alan could be unpredictable and even contradictory, he had knowledge and enthusiasm and built loyalty within his department. He had made strides, but wasn't getting any feedback—until recently, when he discovered things weren't as rosy as they had seemed.

A (Alan): I'm as angry as I've ever been. People are complaining about me, behind my back, to my face, to my boss. I tracked down those complaints and there is no substance to them. They're saying I haven't done things when I have. I told my boss, and it turns out he didn't even know about the feedback. Now he has data that people are upset. I should have just kept my mouth shut. And the other night, one of my former colleagues told me that one of our investors complained I wasn't responsive. These are people I don't even work with any more. They're telling me about this investor who is complaining about a phone message. But the call had only come in Friday night. And it was Saturday. Really? It's a pile-on. There may be no substance there, either. If it was urgent, they have my cell phone. I would answer. This whole thing feels endless. No matter what I do people are annoyed with me. I don't know how to get out from under it. I know I've changed my response time and my time management. I know for a fact it's better.

J (Janet): That's a lot. Can we take these issues one at a time?

A: Yes. Good idea.

I could shine the light somewhere else to reduce his strong Feeling, but zooming in to the source of his anger has merit. Anger has a message, that some value that matters has been thwarted or obstructed. Let's zoom in to that first.

J: When you feel angry about those complaints, what do you think really matters to you?

A: It's like a balloon. I push here, one thing gets better, one thing gets worse.

J: Kind of amorphous, unpredictable?

A: Futile and not fair.

J: And, if you dig under that sense of futility and unfairness, what do you care about that isn't being acknowledged or valued?

A: Lots of things. I care that their information is wrong. I care that I *am* being responsive and not being recognized for it. I care that there are complaints. I've always provided outstanding results, so I care that I'm not being given a break and the benefit of the doubt when there is contradictory information.

J: Would it be accurate to say that you care about accuracy? Quality? Recognition?

A: Yes, definitely: Accuracy and quality are things I care about. And recognition.

Zooming in.

J: When you get closer to noticing how much they matter to you, how do you feel?

A: Oddly, not quite as angry. I've always cared about accuracy and quality, and that's why I'm good at what I do.

J: I'm noticing that bringing those values to mind seems to have reduced your anger somewhat, is that right?

A: Yes, because I know I do those things whether people are aware it or not.

J: You are aligned with yourself in that area.

A: Yes, right.

That doesn't give him an Action yet, but the goal here is to identify the roots of the anger to give him some emotional space—and then some choices—before moving ahead.

J: Okay, shall we look at the next issue?

A: Yes, I'm ready.

I'm zooming in on the next thing he complained about... and his Feeling about it.

J: You mentioned that when you tracked down the issues you didn't find any substance.

A: Right.

J: What bothers you most about that?

A: I don't know where I stand. If there's no substance, what's the storm about?

J: So confusion, uncertainty?

A: Yes.

J: Would you say you value clarity and specificity?

A: What the heck? If there's no lingering unfinished business I owe someone, what's all the fuss? What's it about? Yes, I value clarity—and it's missing.

Time to zoom out from his Feelings now that he has identified them.

J: When you distance yourself from that anger and think about quality, accuracy, clarity and certainty, what do you think about? How do you feel?

A: That's just it. Those are the things I care most about. I feel relieved—to be concrete about that in this moment. To name the things that matter.

J: From that place, how about we do a little planning. Are you ready for that?

A: Yes.

J: Even though some of this feedback seems unfair and some of the residual complaints turn out to be unsubstantiated, you still dislike how these things are impacting your reputation. You would like to change how this is impacting your reputation, correct?

A: Yes.

J: Where else in your life have you felt strongly enough to make a change to your own behavior? You've told me about weight loss.

A: Yeah, but I had to do that twice. Once, my best friend died of a heart attack. My father was over-weight. We have a family history of heart attacks. So I was scared; I lost 45 pounds. Then I put it back on. I woke up one morning and thought, I don't like how I look. I don't like how I feel. I knew how to lose it, so I focused. When I lost half, it felt good, so that kept me going. I can imagine eating what I want to, I can trick my brain into thinking I'm full—even if I've had a small portion.

Changing habits is a challenge, and he knew his own process.

J: What was the strongest motivation?

A: The first time, I felt fear. The second time I was discouraged but the setback also motivated me. What kept me going was that I knew how to reach success; it was more personal, more about my own goals. I knew how to notice the incremental success.

Zooming in to Feeling confident and clear about goals…

J: It's a powerful success strategy because it already contains confidence about what to do if you run into setbacks.

Alan and I then discussed the key players he needed to keep informed. He renewed his commitment to keeping track of requests, emails, and phone calls to be sure he was being as responsive as he intended. Once he was able to zoom in to the strong Feelings and then out to get some distance, Alan had the willingness to develop Action steps. He felt grounded in reconnecting with his own values, and that provided a firm foundation.

Anger is so uncomfortable that many push it aside as a way to control Actions. The ability to control Actions is important, but one shouldn't miss out on the valuable information that anger contains. It needs to be explored in order to expose what is upsetting—and then to develop options and responses. Another reason anger is sometimes neglected is the fear that exploring it will amplify the Feeling and make it worse. In my experience, the opposite occurs: The anger subsides once the source has been acknowledged and given voice.

Pam—Gets Ready to Fire

Pam was a nurse manager in a hospital ICU. She was extremely dedicated to her patients and, by all accounts, a very good nurse. She was a strong communicator with families who were stressed about their loved ones—an additional valuable skill.

Pam was ready to fire Ellie, a relatively new nurse. This is one of the hardest events for most managers, and it *should* be hard and never taken lightly. Managers may have a wide range of complex Feelings, including fear, reluctance, anger, disappointment, and guilt, which keep them on the fence about the process of a termination. Digging in to those Feelings can help identify the options.

One of Pam's goals as a manager is to be more direct and decisive. She tends to bring the same level of compassion to management as she does to her patients, but now she felt torn. In management, compassion needs to be combined with clarity and accountability.

J (Janet): You wanted to talk about Ellie?

P (Pam): I'm ready to tell her, "I think it will not work out."

I want to zoom into the possible mix of Feelings to help Pam get clarity.

J: What's the main thing that's not working out?

P: The patients. Ellie makes mistakes with them. When she's told what she should have done, she gets defensive and blames me or other trusted nurses instead of trying to learn from the experience.

J: So I hear that you're worried about the quality of her patient care?

P: Yes. I've seen too many mistakes. I've really thought about this.

J: I don't hear any ambivalence.

P: No, except, maybe I should watch her some more. I feel like I owe her that.

That went from certainty to uncertainty right away. More exploration is needed.

J: Do you feel that you have enough data—that you're being fair?

P: Yes, but I want to soften the blow. I feel like I owe her that.

On the one hand, I hear that she feels worried about patient care. On the other hand, she is hesitating.

J: What do you owe her?

P: Part of me feels like a hypocrite.

J: Your actions are contradicting your values?

P: I don't know...no.

J: Why might you feel like a hypocrite? What is that feeling?

P: People have helped me, given me second chances. I feel like a hypocrite, taking care of patients but not my own staff.

J: Consider the idea of taking care of her by keeping her. How does that feel?

P: I've seen enough. It's too big a risk. That would feel awful.

J: You feel worried about keeping her?

P: Yes.

J: What matters about compassion and fairness?

P: Having her come in to work for the day just to fire her. That makes me feel mean. But I don't want to do it over the phone, in a text, or in an email. I want her to know why—that she couldn't take feedback and blamed others. Patients are at risk.

J: So the main hesitation is *how* you do it?

P: Yes.

Zooming out to the impact on the group, as well as Ellie...

J: So you've considered the patients and Ellie. How do you feel about how the group will be impacted?

P: They'll be relieved. They've seen the problems, too.

There are many aspects of a termination that can cause anxiety or regret in a manager. When Pam finished reflecting, the main source of her hesitation was due to Feelings she had about the meeting itself, how to structure it, what to say, where and when to hold the meeting, and how to compensate the employee. We practiced ways that felt genuine; compassionate, yet firm. Pam still won't be comfortable with the meeting, but she reconnected with her certainty and aligned with her values. She was ready for the challenge.

Brent—Influence

One of Brent's goals was to not be so defensive. He didn't like the Feeling, and he didn't like the impression it created. He had heard that people describe him that way and wanted to change his reputation.

J (Janet): What would you like to work on today?

B (Brent): I want to manage my relationships better. I don't like that being defensive is now part of my reputation, my brand.

J: What do you know about that tendency?

B: I'm good at my job. I'm thoughtful about how I approach things. I want people to treat me like I'm reliable.

J: So you feel challenged when they question you and worry that it's about your competence?

B: Yes.

I could zoom in on this, but he seems clear on both counts, so I want to find out what Actions he takes and zoom in on Act.

J: Can you give me an example of what you do?

B: Last week, David was checking on my project. People who want something don't realize that I'm always managing multiple projects. I get requests from all over the organization. He asked why wasn't I finished and I barked at him. I know it wasn't professional.

Right off the bat he seems to recognize that his response wasn't appropriate and seems open to improving on his impatient reactions. What's another way he can Act? Let's zoom in on alternative Actions.

J: To help you come up with a different response, can you think about what you wanted to know about David's request?

B: I'd want to know which part mattered most. Maybe there's a segment of the project that he needs right away. Or maybe there's a deadline I'm not aware of. Or pressure from his boss, which I could help mediate.

J: Those sound like great possibilities. What do you think if you were to propose one of them?

B: I can do that. I do want to be responsive. It feels better.

J: So you're lining up how you respond with what you'd really like to do. That seems authentic—it's the real you. Do you agree?

B: Yes.

J: What's an example of when you might have acted this way?

B: I did something like that yesterday when someone wanted me to make a change in a project. Instead of barking at him, I asked more about it—why that change mattered and when he needed it by. Asking like that didn't make me feel frustrated, so I didn't sound frustrated or impatient.

J: Are there other times you want to respond differently?

B: When I'm managing up. I get defensive if I'm asked by my boss or another higher up about my progress on something. I hear it as criticism and run as fast as I can. I resent that pressure.

In this example, I want to zoom out of the Feeling of defensiveness to see if there's a more leveraged Action he could take.

J: If you didn't hear it as criticism, what would you want to know?

B: Why it mattered, I guess. And whether there was a change in priorities. Sometimes executives have lots of conversations about a change in direction on something, and forget they haven't shared them. It's so familiar to them they don't realize we don't know.

He's already been able to zoom into a possible cause of a communication breakdown, and zoom out enough to not take it personally. That's the first step to take in avoiding being defensive.

J: What is your reaction when you consider zooming out of the feeling of defensiveness to get some perspective on causes?

B: I like it. It feels less stressful.

J: What might you ask?

B: Just that—whether there's a change in direction. Can I learn more about what he's inquiring about? It could just be interest, not criticism. It could be he wants my opinion about a change he's considering. It maybe he's just being collegial.

Alternative interpretations are reducing his Feelings of defensiveness.

J: Can you think of another managing up situation?

B: Yes, my one-on-one meetings with my manager often get rescheduled. I get frustrated, but you know what? I'm going to ask that we move those standing meetings to an earlier time. I don't think they'll be canceled as often, and I won't need to feel frustrated.

J: Great, that sounds actionable.

B: I never get any feedback on my monthly summaries. My boss asks me for them, and I write them. Then I just don't know what happens next.

I zoom out just a bit from his not getting a response, and Feeling resentful perhaps, to the option of another action...

J: You're on a roll. What do you want to do differently?

B: It's so obvious. I can just bring the monthly summaries to our one-on-ones and ask for feedback. I could make that agenda item number one.

J: Great. Can you think of any other defensiveness issues?

B: Well, it's related—but I think it's more along the lines of influence. I run a cross-functional project and a related meeting for updates. Sometimes people are really stubborn and stuck in their ways. Dead-set even. I need new strategies.

Zooming in...

J: For example?

B: (Describes a new project update procedure he is creating.) All I get is pushback. I'm just trying to streamline things.

Zooming in to Feelings...

J: How do you feel when that happens?

B: Defensive—like they think I haven't thought it through even though I have. I also feel disrespected. Can't they just go along with it?

J: Good to know. Now that you've identified your feelings and that you were being defensive, what do you know about their resistance?

B: Not a lot, so obviously the first step I should try is to find out more. Ask more. What would be challenging about the new procedure? What's in the way? I'd be more clear about why I proposed it, too.

He is already zooming in to learn more and zooming out to get his own big picture.

Through I series of questions I guide Brent to move in closer or further away from his Feelings which helped him identify Actions he could take. I also try to help them recognize and understand the impact of his Actions on others: the feelings they may create.

In today's business world, emotions are increasingly out in the open and work environments are taking note. Businesses are recognizing that emotions are an undeniable ingredient of the human drama. Feelings are an important and valid source of information and, more often than not, they are in charge of behavior rather than logic. Bringing some respect to this dimension is not just polite or "good business," it's a potential source of powerful intuition. Leaders who cultivate an awareness of their emotions are better able to interpret and regulate them. They are better able to demonstrate empathy, which improves relationships with management, staff, and customers.

AJ was able to connect with disappointment and anger over the fact that his qualitative contributions were not recognized in the face of missing his quantitative targets. That motivated him to be more outspoken in the future when he felt the expectations were unreasonable, or established without sufficient data. It also motivated him to lobby for more recognition for building toward long-term results—even if short-term numbers were missed. His anger informed him.

Often strong performers, such as Pat, have a confidence that can belie uncertainty. Feelings of confidence can be so wrapped up in competence that it can feel personal when one is challenged. Pat was fortunate to have caught herself in the act of defensiveness and that she had a manager who recognized her ability to grow in this area. In determining to develop this new reaction, her insight about a software metaphor sustained her confidence.

Like many high performers, Connie's inner bully had demanded commitment and results. This may have motivated her to successful achievement up until that point, but it was now interfering. She was aware that she was overly anxious without a lot of supporting data. Getting some distance from that inner critic and reframing the context to be more hospitable may help her gain some equanimity in order to build skills, which will in turn lead to increased confidence.

Pedro had a process of reflecting on his irritation, which eventually led to insights. While he didn't always have clarity on the exact sources or remedy for his discomfort, he knew enough to allow it to marinate while he figured it out. His Feelings ultimately revealed clear next steps, leading to congruence with his values.

Many executives have an inner bulldog—a part of them that is insistent, aggressive, and goal-driven. Often this creates impressive results. Raphael had benefited from this approach in a challenging, regulated industry. He recognized that his goal was to win; while this had some commendable benefits, it was coming at the expense of constructive relationships with his partners. Although he struggles with ambivalence about having to make a change in his communication style, he is goal-oriented enough to focus on improved harmony as a desirable result. That way he builds more choices into his range of reactions. When the "bulldog" is truly needed, it's still handy for him. When the situation requires him to be collegial, he can begin to feel more confident with that behavior.

Ron was feeling frustrated because his good work was not enough. His management style—specifically his flexibility about scheduling—was negatively affecting his reputation. When a leader feels that his Action is completely appropriate, it is especially difficult to take on the challenge of change. His resentment took center stage at first, but then he recognized that he may have been unconsciously managing in a way to create an adrenaline rush. That kind of excitement can be as addictive as caffeine. He realized that his old rhythm of working was not worth the reputation cost.

Alan was feeling constantly criticized and unable to pin down the source of people's dissatisfaction. This uncertainty can raise the stress level so high that clear thinking is elusive. In his case he was ignoring inquiries, emails, and phone calls in an unconscious attempt to distance from the criticism. That predictably ended in a negative result. Alan was able to draw on past success models to remind himself of his own determination, commitment, and resilience, and ability to make change.

For many good reasons, terminating an employee is generally fraught with anxiety. It is risky on many levels, and Pam had several Feelings competing against her need to terminate. Separating them out and digging in to each helped her identify what was most prominent for her to focus on, which led to clear next steps.

Brent's defensiveness was a problem, and he knew it. Digging in to the sources gave him the ability to consider alternative actions.

5

Lens Four—Witness

The concept of "Witness" may not sound very corporate to most people who work in that type of environment. Companies are action-oriented; they are sources of productivity. Witnessing can sound passive. Witness involves simply letting people discover something important for themselves; it involves being there for them, being a caring listener, and sometimes a mirror to reflect back thoughts. It provides the opportunity for someone to think out loud and explore inner contradictions, paradoxes, or clarity. It may be thought of as presence or active listening. Active listening is the ability to hear someone without preparing a response while they are talking. It includes suspending judgment, and concentrating to fully understand their meaning and point of view. Active listening includes acknowledging the speaker's meaning, whether in body language or in a verbal summary of what was significant for them. It may be experienced as empathy or support. It is a rare and wonderful experience. Feeling deeply understood can be profoundly meaningful; it has the power to restore and renew someone's energy or sense of self.

Witness can feel passive for the listener; it takes patience, but it can be extremely empowering for the individual being heard. It provides the space for someone to explore what is deeply important or become aware of a contribution or legacy that yearning to be noticed or manifested. Creating an opportunity for someone to be revealed to him or herself may require that they be revealed to someone else. Witnessing someone's longing, reflection, disappointment, or resolution is a powerful moment. Offering the time to allow these thoughts to emerge and take form becomes deeply meaningful for both parties.

Integrating a major change such as a promotion, losing a long-time boss or peer, or an unexpected death of a colleague takes up psychic space and energy—whether it's a positive or negative occurrence. This space and energy needs to be provided for and witnessed with care. In my opinion, it needs to be occur much more often in the workplace. It takes a supportive witness to cope with extreme emotion: worry, outrage, grieving, resolve, excitement. Making time for this narrative is a gift; a healing step amidst our fast-paced world of deadlines and deliverables. The experience of being deeply heard will be cherished long after the details of the conversation are forgotten.

To help work through changes and transitions, some individuals may practice mindfulness: a practice of learning to be a witness to oneself through meditation, yoga, or silence. Others may go on retreats to create the space and time to listen to their inner dialogue and discover inner truth. Some companies may hold organized management retreats for the purpose of getting out of the day-to-day to plan for the year or more. To reflect on what matters, what the company stands for, and whether it is living into its mission. In the same way, each member of that management team needs renewal.

Jogging, hiking, or painting are other ways one may find renewal. Some people have a spiritual community, a men's or women's group, or a prayer group that meets this need. All of these forums foster contemplative time to explore one's inner calling.

I am always honored to be present when I Witness a leader stepping into this reflective space. Focusing your attention for the sole purpose of understanding can be reassuring, supportive, and even life-changing for both parties.

It helps to be mindful of yourself and whether you are able to provide this to another person. Make sure you will not be distracted by a pressing mental or emotional issue. In the middle of a busy day of heavy demands and office and family problems, it can be difficult to move into that place of peaceful presence. Sometimes meditating in advance may help prepare you clear your head and offer the benefit of deep listening.

Mind-Clearing Meditation

Occasionally I have a client who has lost his or her way mentally or emotionally after a major occurrence or change. They have lost their connection to their own inner truth or values. The following meditation came to me while I was n an airplane to meet a client, Scott. It may have been meant for him that day, but it proved so effective that I've offered it to other leaders since then.

Take a deep breath and a long exhale. Take another breath and an exaggerated exhale out, clearing out the old air. Notice the rise and fall of your chest, the air as it enters your lungs. Bring all of your attention to your breath, the air going in and out of your nose. At the same time, bring all of your attention to your diaphragm and your lungs; follow the rise and fall of each breath. Notice how relaxed you can be when you make time for breathing.

Imagine yourself on a mountain and you are climbing higher and higher. Imagine the sun on your back, the effort and exertion. Imagine the challenge and the peace that comes from being so absorbed in a task. Allow yourself to be totally present in that task, noticing only the satisfaction of the process. Continue on up the mountain, higher and higher along the paths and over tree trunks. Enjoy the beauty of the ruggedness. Once you are at the top of the mountain, relax even deeper into your experience.

While still at top of the mountain, notice the warm soothing feeling of the sun all around you; soak in the golden light, and let that awareness remind you of your own worthiness. Let the sun's golden light be a reminder that you are here for a reason, entwined with all those you know, work with, or even meet casually.

Now I'd like you to look across at the next mountain peak and see another you—over there on that mountain peak. Be aware of your importance to all those who love you. Now—bring into existence in the image each one of your family members, so you are surrounded by people who care about you. Send them appreciation and love, as represented by the sun's rays. Next—bring to mind extended family members, cousins, and in-laws and send them love and appreciation. Call on your grandparents, great grandparents, and other ancestors living and dead and send them loving appreciation. Envision your teachers, bosses, and mentors who have helped you along the path and send them appreciation. Imagine friends you have known and cared about and send them loving appreciation. Bring into the scene friends who have been challenging to you, or have somehow disappointed you, and appreciate what you have learned from these experiences. Invite people who for some reason are no longer in your life, and appreciate them as well. Relax into the awareness of being interconnected with all those employees who enable your organization to provide its mission and services to the world. Now let the mountain be filled with the many others whose lives you have touched; send them your good wishes that their lives may be enhanced by your past contact with them.

It's now time to relax into the experience of holding all those people in your heart. Focus on your good intentions and all the ways in which these individuals aspire to be worthy of your appreciation. Take a few minutes until you have relaxed into the fullness of all those you wish well—all of those who have benefited by their association with you or have been touched by you.

Once you have experienced the fullness of this, give a nod and allow your inner wisdom to offer an image or sensation—a picture or word so you can recall it. Once you have this locked, give it another nod.

Now I'd like you to notice all those good wishes you have been sending out to others. Have them all send good wishes to you, knowing they would want this to be mutual, to be shared. These family members, friends, colleagues, and acquaintances have all been moved or helped in some way by something you have said or done. Employees current and past receive their appreciation, even though they may never know you personally. Hone in on your co-workers and boss, and receive their appreciation for your helpfulness and good cheer. Receive good wishes from relatives and ancestors who have died, who are grateful for all you do and for continuing their legacy. Receive loving appreciation from your relatives, drinking the joyful love of your immediate and extended family. Let yourself fill up with peaceful receiving. Release any resistance to receiving this appreciation. If you have any resistance remaining, let this version of you smile with gentle knowing and understanding and let go of it, relaxing fully into receiving appreciation.

As you are now ready to merge this with the original you on the first mountain, let your inner wisdom offer you an image or word to help you preserve the peaceful noticing of this state; once you have this, give a nod. Once you have allowed this image or word to become a recognizable symbol, merge together the two parts—the one on the other mountain with you on the first mountain. Relax into the peace of knowing you are so connected, supported, and appreciated. As you wish the best for others, know that you are surrounded by people who care about you and also wish you the best.

Discovering Silence

Remembering to give plenty of space and silence is a key element when choosing to offer the gift of Witness. The individual expressing him or herself needs to Feel deeply understood, which benefits the speaker, the Witness, and perhaps colleagues back at the office. Bearing Witness in this way can be received as a loving act—even while corporate boundaries remain safely in place. Bearing witness fills me with awe. To watch someone unfold to his or her inner truth is a beautiful event, as inspiring and mysterious as a sunset. Alison Gopnick describes awe as "that special sense of the vastness of nature, the universe, the cosmos." She goes on to quote researcher Prof. Dacher Keltner's research on awe. The effect is to shrink our egos, create greater connection to others, and expand our sense of well-being.

Psychologist Paul Piff says, "Having a little bit of awe every day in your life would make you happier, kinder and more compassionate."

Nathan's New Job

Nathan was a former client I had worked with several years ago. I knew he had joined a health care data start-up as accounting director. He really had wanted the title of chief financial officer, but the founders—two brothers who were graduates from a prestigious Boston business college—had assured him that the promotion would be his after he proved himself.

Less than a year later, the investors were willing to consider providing another round of financing. As a condition, they insisted on a more seasoned chief executive officer. They brought in an executive over the founders who had previously shared the CEO role. This was a big disappointment for Nathan, who really liked the energy and mission of the young founders. They were innovative and personable; confident without being arrogant. They invited input from others. Although the company was not yet profitable, they were in it for the long haul; they sought to change the industry with their data. They weren't just looking for a short stint with quick profit and genuinely cared about what they were creating. It occurred to Nathan that, with the new infusion of investor capital, the company might be in a position to go public in the next few years. This would be a great experience and he knew that Bob, the new CEO, had been through initial public offerings before. Nathan recognized that he could learn a lot from him.

A year or so after Bob was brought on Nathan called me for a session. He had just received his performance review and was extremely agitated. He needed to get his emotions out.

> N (Nathan): I can't believe the performance review Bob gave me. I've done everything they asked. I have the skills they need.

> J (Janet): What were his comments?

> N: I'm used to great reviews. He was critical. Something about relationships. And that some of my financial projects had become too complex. But hey, finance is complex, and I knew that every budget had to be really accurate; we operated close to the bone. And when it comes to relationships, don't forget: These are all scientists and mathematicians. They don't listen to each other. It's true, the senior management team could do a better job communicating—but that's everyone. Not just me.

> *He is not asking for a new perspective or insight, he is just creating a narrative for his own experience. I am Witnessing his process.*

> J: So the entire team has communication issues?

> N: Yes, and we have people from all over the world. That adds to the challenge. You can't tell what people's assumptions are, but there are plenty of disconnects. Some of it is language—people from other countries

whose first language is not English. Some of it is jargon—the science or computer folks. Some of it is tunnel vision—only seeing their own departments' issues. We have lots of young people and that's great—great for energy. But energy isn't enough to run a company.

J: How did the team operate?

N: Well, that's just it. Bob didn't even call management team meetings until he'd been here almost six months. Don't you think *that's* a relationship problem?

J: It sounds like his management style was a disappointment to you.

I'm Thinking Nathan needs to air his Feelings and sense of unfairness. This is not the time to create a learning strategy.

N: Yes, it was disappointing. He brought in his old buddies one by one this past year. Guys he had worked with before. If there was a conflict, he sided with them. How am I supposed to get a fair hearing?

He was understandably focused on the recent meeting. I wasn't sure if he was ready to zoom out to the bigger context. This cannot be rushed; it must go at the client's pace.

J: What would be helpful to working with Bob?

N: I need to think about if I know what he wants me to do differently—and if I even care. If I have the energy to change. I need to think about if I need to be in an environment where my skills are acknowledged. I think I would have been regarded as more of a key player if I'd insisted on the more senior title and role when I first joined. Now I regret that I was not more assertive when

I accepted the initial offer—but, as I say, I felt a real rapport with the founders.

While I am tempted to zoom in to or out of his discomfort, his venting energy tells me this is a time to just Witness. He has strong emotions and it is not yet time to work on new perspectives or self-reflection. We spent the rest of the time on his reaction to the review, which he perceived as unfair and not substantive. He felt the review did not acknowledge his skills and contributions.

Several months later, Nathan called to tell me the good news that he had a new job. The new company's CEO had offered him a controller role with the promise of a promotion once he had proven himself. He said this was not his first rodeo and that the CFO title was a condition of accepting the offer. They met his requirement of the CFO title.

Nathan and I had lunch and he is doing fine in his new role. He enjoys working for this company, respects its leadership, and currently does not need coaching. He says that our session from months earlier was reassuring. Although he remembers how agitated he felt at the time, it was essential for him to be able to express his frustrations to me in a non-judgmental environment. Hearing his own thoughts about it enabled him to realize that he and Bob were not going to see eye-to-eye no matter what he did, and he was tired of trying to prove himself there.

Being recognized for his twenty years in finance was important to his career, self-esteem, and sense of making a difference. He wants to build a legacy by contributing to companies in healthcare, thereby healthcare in general. All of this provides him with a meaningful sense of purpose.

Simon's New Project

Simon was a software developer in a biotech company. I already had a few sessions with Simon, and he made significant changes in a short amount of time. His goals were to be more aware of his staff's status on projects and be more informed when it came time to report up to his manager, Doug.

> J (Janet): What is your update?
>
> S (Simon): I've been experimenting with different ways of meeting. What's been working is my having one-on-one meetings with each of my managers. It would be great if we could do that every week, but it's just not realistic. Instead we meet every other week.
>
> J: What's working well about that arrangement?
>
> S: It lets me be informed about what they're working on, and also I can give them tips and mentor them about delegating to their team members.
>
> J: Sounds like that's effective for you.
>
> S: I've also added monthly meetings with the entire group: my managers and their team members. I have each person give a ten-minute update one meeting. At the next meeting, we invite people in other departments to share their priorities and direction.
>
> J: Great. So what is helpful about that format?
>
> *Simon is pleased with what is working, so there is no need to change perspective or focus.*
>
> S: It keeps all of us informed. There's a subtle peer accountability because they have to report progress. And it helps us stay on course in the context of our stakeholders.

J: Excellent. Anything else?

S: Yes, there is something I want to think through. I've been putting off going upstairs to talk to my manager's manager about funding a new project.

J: What have you noticed about that?

S: It's easy enough for me to go upstairs. The fact that I haven't done it tells me there is something I'm avoiding.

I'm Witnessing his self-awareness.

J: Why might that be?

S: I feel under pressure to do my work. I guess I don't think of using my time in that way as real work. Maybe that's it. I like working on things that have concrete results. Things that are at a more granular level. I'm not sure I think that "going upstairs" is real work.

J: So you're avoiding having a funding conversation?

S: Yes and no. I'm actually excited at the prospect of having the new project funded. Speaking to the executives is kind of exciting; it holds a lot of promise. Maybe I'm stuck in the feeling of anticipation. I like the anticipation. It feels like going on vacation. Anticipation is half the fun.

Simon is already being reflective, aware of multiple currents, so I'm just going to Witness and hold up the mirror.

J: Sounds like you're aware of what is holding you back. Anything else?

S: Yes, I'm aware of the political undercurrents. I want to make sure I know where they stand on what I'm about to ask them about. I don't want to go in blind. I want to know how to prepare my business case. In the past couple of days, I've learned where James stands, which has encouraged me more. Now I feel ready to talk with him.

J: It sounds like one source of apprehension was that you were lacking information, and you have discovered that information. It's good to know what reduces anxiety for you. What else do you need in order to take action?

S: I'm puzzled. I generally feel quite empowered to open these conversations. I don't want to get too psychotherapeutic babble about it—but maybe fear of success. When I think about how Bob might respond, I expect he'll be enthused.

J: If he becomes enthused, how bad would that be?

S: *(Laughing)*. It wouldn't be bad at all, except that I'd have to—then I'd get to do the new project.

He still sounded anxious, caught himself saying "have to" and changed it to "get to." I wanted to zoom into the possibility of getting approval for the new project.

J: Sometimes ambivalence can come from a values conflict. What possibilities do you think of with regard to the new project?

S: I would like to do the new project, but I would really want others involved. On the one hand, I have the value of personal productivity; on the other is teamwork. Now that I think of it, that's another thing I wanted to explore today.

J: You want to think about how much individual work you do?

S: Yes. I feel responsible for doing my own work. It makes it hard to make time for the management part and the fund requests to upper management.

This is a common difficulty as managers get promoted. Managing and other management tasks, such as budgeting and meetings, don't feel like real work. Time to zoom out a little and shine the light to include that.

J: What if you included funding, delegating, meeting, and communicating with leadership as all falling within your job. What if each one of those *counts* as real work?

S: That make sense. I don't know if I can get used to that view of it. I've always been proud of my own software code.

Simon had mostly done his own work regarding reflection and awareness. For this reason, my role during most of the session my job was to be a Witness. When he spoke about his dilemma about individual work vs. management work, we zoomed out to include all of his responsibilities, which may help him give himself credit for the management piece. Every level of promotion takes some getting used to, and it's important to recognize that managing others is real work in terms of planning, talent development, strategy, and scalability. More can be done when managing productive, motivated managers and staff.

Ashley—Sense of Mission

Ashley had been hopeful about her job when she joined about a year ago, but found herself losing interest and not feeling engaged. One of her complaints was that she felt like an outsider, as she was the newest member in a seven-person organization. She didn't feel integrated into the business; others would leave her out of key information, such as notifying her of an upcoming big meeting so she could be prepared to greet visitors.

Another complaint was that her boss, Irene, was non-emotive. Ashley found Irene cool, detached, and unenthusiastic; she didn't even seem to be mission-driven in a pretty mission-driven social services organization. This disconnect was damaging their connection: Ashley so passionate, whereas Irene acted cool. It didn't have to end the connection, but Ashley felt adrift, alienated.

> A (Ashley): I was so excited when I started here. I had hopes and expectations about being able to make a difference. But now I just feel like an outsider. I'm not in the heart of the business—and we're so small. I could be, I should be! I'm wearing too many undefined hats to be able to make a significant contribution in any one area. I get the leftovers to do. I don't really own any area of work. I'm losing interest. Each day drags.

> J: It must be difficult to come in to work with that feeling.

> A: Especially since Irene was the reason I joined—and now I just don't get her.

> *I know it is time to zoom out and shine the light on the other end of the spectrum. I had heard Irene's weaknesses from Ashley's point of view, but I'm also aware that she and others deeply appreciate her.*

> J: Given that you find your boss Irene to be detached, remote, inaccessible, and cool—if those are her weaknesses, what traits are well developed? What does she do well?

> A: I've seen her with clients and families. She's unflappable and even-tempered.

I'm still zooming out. Since she mentioned that clients value and appreciate the boss, I wonder what they see in her.

J: Would you be able to be in the room when she's dealing with others so you could see what happens when they appreciate her?

A: I have seen her, and I've seen that positive response. I'm not sure what it is.

J: What is your own reaction to seeing others appreciate her?

A: It's nice. I'm glad they do. Her charisma is part of what drew me here. But I really miss living the mission.

J: Can you tell me more about that?

A: We're committed to personal relationships and improving lives. That's what we do. And we're not doing it in an ordinary everyday way with each other.

J: That seems like a big loss. Anything else?

A: I think of myself as being more head-based than heart-based.

J: If you see your own style as head-based, could that have anything to do with your negative judgment of Irene's coolness?

I think it is time to zoom out and see what Ashley and Irene might have in common. If they are both head-based more than heart-based, where is the disconnect? I'm wondering if Ashley is self-critical about being more head-based.

A: I don't think so.

J: From how you describe what you do, you seem to be comfortable with logic and analytical skills. It seems to me that you are also empathic, caring, and mission-driven—all qualities associated with a heart-based orientation. Do you see yourself that way?

A: Yes, definitely.

J: And that's part of what drew you here?

A: Yes, I had returned to graduate school to deepen my knowledge about blended and adoptive families, and this job seemed like a good foot in the door.

J: You were hoping to make a contribution to families in this situation?

A: Yes, it can have such a huge impact on a person's development. On a family's well being.

J: And here you are—in a way, in a microcosm: the non-profit version of a blended work family, so to speak.

A: Yeah, maybe that's it. That feeling of being a step-child in this work environment.

J: That seems like a pretty profound mirroring of the very situation this agency is designed to help.

A: Maybe that's it!

I'm zooming using her personal discomfort to explore whether this experience might be able to inform her. Could it be part of her personal research? Could her insights potentially ignite the agency? Or at least, be an experience from which she could learn?

J: If there was some redeeming feature to your discomfort and disenchantment—and it was that you could

identify with the experience of your client population—
what possibilities open up for you?

Her eyes lit up at the possibility that her hurt could be recycled into useful information that could potentially change the way the agency offered services—or at least inform her professionally moving forward.

In this scenario I had zoomed out to Witness, helping to support her exploration about meaning and purpose in her life and work. The session ended in a beautiful kind of silence.

Barbara—Balance

Barbara was a client in line for promotion, and we had been meeting for several months when we had this session. She is hardworking and effective and, on this day, became reflective about what she really wants.

> B (Barbara): I need more work life balance. We have a place on the Cape. I love it, especially off-season. It takes me a while to unwind at the end of the day. Getting away helps. I need more time in serenity. I feel burned out.

> J (Janet): What gives you serenity?

> B: Yoga, hiking, kayaking. My kids are teenagers now, so they are much more independent. It's hard to even get them to join us on a family outing. So my husband and I do outdoorsy things—just the two of us, unless the kids decide to come. I really like that. It helps me clear my mind. I need more serenity before I can step back and think about my overall goals.

> J: What keeps you from having more of that kind of time?

B: It's not the job's fault. It's not my boss's fault. It's partly the role—all the meetings before and after work. It's also my own rhythm, my own work ethic. I can't turn it off.

She has already shared that she is Witness to her own role in the dilemma.

J: What's one small thing you can add that would give you a bit more serenity?

B: Reading helps—especially novels. I travel in my mind, to a completely different place and time. I can get so lost in it, I can't even get to sleep until I read what's next. And I know these aren't real people.

She knows what she needs: I'm just Witnessing.

J: You told me you recently negotiated a deadline extension with your boss—that's another good way to provide self-care.

B: Yeah, when I remember to do that—and don't feel too guilty about it.

J: Do you feel guilty?

B: I know that's self-imposed. My reputation here is solid. It's crazy, though, I told my husband I didn't want to go to the Cape this weekend because I wanted to finish preparing for a presentation. I thought getting that done would provide me with serenity. And it worked. I did it on Saturday and then my mind was clear. Since I didn't go with him and the kids to the Cape, Sunday was peaceful. I don't get a lot of alone time. It was nice to have the house to myself. I know it sounds crazy—that I'd rather work than get away.

J: It doesn't have to make sense to others. Just to you. You knew what you needed.

B: I don't get thinking time at work. I help not only my own staff, but people from other departments march right in. They'll complain about a new process, about their boss or co-worker. Maybe because I've been here so long. I don't know why everyone comes to us. They sit right down. I do care—maybe that's why. I guess they know I'll do something if I can. But I can't take on everyone's issues. It makes my brain noisy all the time. I need to be more neutral, not get so reactive about helping everyone.

J: Anything else that would give you relief?

B: Be more of a resource and less of a martyr. I can feel it when resentment creeps in. And that's my own fault.

She is really providing her own new perspectives.

J: Great to be aware of it. Anything else?

B: I want to see if I can compartmentalize—if I can be at work when I'm here, and not have work on my mind when I'm home. I want to notice what energizes me, and what creates serenity. I'd like to figure out what wears me down and stop doing it.

J: That sounds like a useful process.

B: Maybe I could influence more. The complaints that come here are real. They are process problems. I don't own them, but I do see them. Once I catch my breath, maybe I can suggest a high level meeting, to look at those preventively. Influence solutions without owning them.

Barbara realized she wanted to develop a new habit, a fresh way of dealing with employees. She had been promoted because she was knowledgeable and personable, but had found that the constant demands by others were draining her. Although she was ambitious, she was Thinking of the solution in terms of time off, time at her vacation home. As she thought through the pressures, Witnessed them, she realized there were other ways she could gain equilibrium, in addition to her well-earned time off.

Charlotte—Strategic View

Charlotte was a seasoned manager who had built strong relationships with her staff. She was feeling overwhelmed and was quite aware that Nancy, her manager and company CEO, was feeling overwhelmed, too. This was making everyone edgy. One of Charlotte's goals was to be more strategic—in her own role and in her relationship with her manager. Nancy had also defined one of Charlotte's goals as making better distinctions about priorities and urgencies; she shouldn't consider everything to be urgent.

> C (Charlotte): Years ago, we were small, collegial. Everyone was hands-on. Now our CEO, Nancy, doesn't want to be so hands-on. That's appropriate—but she is knowledgeable, and everyone feels like they know her. Anyone can drop by her office or even call her at home—especially the long-timers. They think she may have some insight they don't want to miss—or some strong opinion that they don't want to go against. She doesn't have anything left in her bucket. She's depleted. And she has a challenging adult child to contend with once she gets home at the end of the day. I get maxed out, too. I close my door. I never used to have to do that. My staff comes in all the time. I realize that's my fault—not theirs. When we were smaller, we were informal like that. People were learning their roles and getting to know each other. But many of them

have been here a long time now. They know their jobs. I'm beginning to believe that they come to me more out of habit rather than really needing an answer. I have to be clear about what's ok with me. I need to do the same with my manager. I realize I go to Nancy when maybe I don't really need to. We both need to learn to set ground rules—and then apply them.

Charlotte has zoomed out on a time line and zoomed back in, being able to see how the present changes the context. She is well aware of her Feelings and her part in the dynamic that she wants to change. She is able to Witness herself.

J (Janet): Is that more in line with what you would like?

C: Yes, that's the irony. I want more space. Sometimes I feel like Nancy micromanages me. But that's my own fault. I go to her with things I can handle, just to keep her in the loop. That leaves her with the impression I'm not strategic. And I allow my staff to come to me with things they can handle. It's the same dynamic, pointed both ways.

She is zoomed in to the details but she wants to be zoomed out to focus on the big picture.

J: What do you think she means by being more strategic?

C: Right now, I have two new hires. We have some policy changes, and I want to be careful about how they are rolled out—how they impact my staff—make sure the new folks are on board. She sees that as me protecting my people, not having the good of the whole company in mind. But I don't think that's fair. I think taking care of each individual ends up taking care of the whole—especially with high producers, such as two people on my staff. Those are the ones we *should* protect. Other people dump work in my department.

Zooming into the word dump, as it generally indicates a Feeling of resentment.

J: Can you say more about that?

C: The roles aren't clear enough. We become the dumping ground. If something falls in the gray area, we get it. It makes me feel queasy.

I want to zoom into that Feeling a little. Queasy is not a common business word.

J: What can you tell me about that queasy feeling?

C: Seasick. Walking a little lopsided. Like I don't quite know which way gravity is pulling. And I'm swaying from side-to-side to try to get my bearings.

J: What do you know about the cause of that?

C: Like when the rug is pulled out from under me. Having agreements one day about policy and procedure, and then people change them without all the decision-makers in the room.

Zooming closer...

J: Anything else?

C: Also, having too many openings without enough recruiting help. When we're short-staffed all those thoughtful plans go out the window. It feels as if I'm just grabbing for things like they were flying objects to keep them from landing and breaking.

She strikes me as being clear and articulate about the root cause and the Feelings they create.

J: Let's see if we can get a little distance from that. If you were to use that strategy lens and imagine that it's three months from now, what do you see?

C: Ideally, I'm fully staffed. I've succeeded in conveying to my staff that they are capable, competent, and don't need to come to me as much. I've stuck with that and backed their decisions, so they have the experience and I trust them.

J: How does that feel?

C: That feels good. Since my staff can handle the day-to-day, I don't feel so scattered and torn and I can think about the whole company. I can care about strategy and other departments and how we work together. And you know what? If they dump stuff on us, I'll make sure that the flow of work is the right one for the company. I'm okay with conflict—let's have it out. I'll have the presence of mind to challenge and reflect. If my department should be handling that, then the headcount and resources should follow. I can deal with the extra work as long as we can do it well. I just want it to be clear and have agreed upon by everyone.

I hear that she's ready to zoom into an Act. She is Witness to her own process and abilities.

J: What would create that?

C: I need a road map. I don't really need my manager's help, I can do it. I need her buy-in, of course, but once I benefit from her experience I can create the roadmap and just do it. I'll set metrics, define the role, and the areas of accountability to achieve the results.

Once Charlotte had surfaced what was on her mind, she was able to walk through her priorities and options. She had high energy and was able to outline her next steps. Her strong Feelings informed her, but didn't overwhelm her in any lasting way. They provided the impetus for her to recreate what she needed. My role in this session was to Witness her internal process.

Gregor—Job Satisfaction

Gregor was an experienced leader with whom I had worked on and off over many years in various roles with different companies. At this time, he is working with an international organization, where he is responsible for running several programs. The organization is facing a change in focus and funding, which could affect his role. He opens by reflecting on the decision-making style of Jerry, his manager.

> G (Gregor): The way Jerry runs an organization is unorthodox: the way he funds it, the way he partners with other organizations, and the way he makes decisions. If we both have the same objective, we tend to arrive at the same place independently. It could be the intrinsic logic of the business problem—we're both very logical. We analyze them the same way.

> J (Janet): Does that provide some comfort?

> G: Not automatically—all of this change could be a black hole. Then I remember that Jerry and I often arrive at the same conclusion, and I'm fine. I've managed to maintain equanimity around the pending changes, specifically to my role. I can't imagine it will be a disaster. I have a lot of confidence in my abilities. These tools we've discussed are helpful, too. Remembering to think short-term and long-term, get closer to the details and look further out to the whole organization. I'm not overly concerned about working with difficult people, provided I have a few tools in my kit

for dealing with them. It's not the end of the world for me if I'm facing difficulty. I'm not that conflict averse.

He's noticing what he's Thinking, and then how that leads to his Feeling of equanimity. He is his own Witness.

J: I see that sometimes this has been a strength of yours.

G: I'm pursuing the projects in my territories with more deliberation. I have eager workers in some cities where allowing a more organic unfolding would be more appropriate. My first instinct is to be directive, but without using that tendency I've been able to say, "We can let this one evolve." I've done that consistently—better than in past. Explain myself. Every time I suggest whether we do something or not I explain why and provide my thinking behind it. I'm concerned about a misstep with an affiliate. In every case the response I get is fairly consistent. They say, "Okay—I see, fine." People really respond well when I explain my thinking to them. That's working for me. I've also been pressured to do things on a hurry up basis. I've resisted this when I didn't think it was the best way to go.

He's describing how he Thinks, which affects how he Acts.

J: Your reputation for urgency may have provided a foundation for that acceptance.

G: It seems to be working: Responses are consistently in general agreement with my recommendations. I'm happy that I'm practicing these skills. It's helping not just me; it's also been working for my relationship with staff.

J: How have you helped your staff?

G: I've found I like the mentoring. This approach puts me in a position of trusted advisor. It's a different role than boss or co-worker. Some staff members are fairly new at what they're doing. Sharing my expertise makes everything more enjoyable.

J: Sounds like a win-win.

G: I've been evolving my communication style managing up as well. I call it "lighter tough." I'm lighter in my delivery—in the frequency and style of communication—but tough in my confident stand. I've used that approach in taking on new assignments.

He's noticing how he is Thinking about how he's Acting, and the impact of that change.

J: In what way?

G: I used to feel overloaded. I have a strong work ethic and it can be difficult for me to deflect, rethink, or renegotiate an assignment. But I've reframed it to think of my role as triage. Instead of automatically accepting an assignment, I'll triage it and see whether I'm the best one—or if it can be scoped differently. I was probably unnecessarily overloading myself on occasion. That's a valuable lesson learned. Not everything is equally important.

He has been able to be Witness to his old habit and make adjustments.

J: Has that also added to your job satisfaction?

G: You can make your own job satisfaction. I think you're probably getting the theme: I feel like I'm in control. It's almost an effortless kind of control. Things are not as difficult as they were; conflicts don't arise as frequently. I'm respectful of relationships, more mindful. Problems I might have had in the past just don't come up anymore. I don't have to deal with them. I don't have to have a strategy.

He's describing that his Action is one of Feeling in control of how he Thinks and Feels.

J: What's an example?

G: Slowing the pace of my decision-making and interactions is having that effect. I'm just not rushed. Not thinking of what I'm going to say next. For example, there's a new guy in Miami who started this week. I was about to send an email—a list of things he should know and do as part of his orientation. I stopped myself. I don't know him. Getting to know him would be more important than these bits of data. Instead, I suggested a short call by phone or that I come to meet him—one to two days, if he'd like. I'm taking the relationship part of this seriously.

J: You're actually responding to the need under the need. You're orienting him not just in terms of facts and framework, but also to help him get his bearings.

G: He may not know how much he has to learn to make things happen—how we work together, our *Modus agendi*. How do we cooperate as a team to do this? He knows mission and that's it. I want to give the personal touch, so I'll go and visit with him. This is in stark contrast to how I got off on wrong foot with the guy in London. Granted, it was more difficult to meet with him face-to-face. I made a lot of assumptions about our working relationship—and shouldn't have. He didn't take it well. I invested no time at all to figure out who he was and where he came from. I didn't place value in the working relationship. I might have been better off to practice a lighter touch with him.

J: It's to your credit that you've designed this different approach.

G: It worked with Ellen. She felt that she was left out of the loop when she was away for two weeks. Before things escalated I brought her into the loop. She seemed to calm down as I filled her in. I felt relief when it was over. This had the potential to damage our working relationship, but I had enough presence of mind to treat her complaint not as an attack but a request for help. My linear thinking serves me well in many cases, but work relationships are often more complicated than figuring out how to get from point A to point B. My old way of thinking was: How can I defend myself? Now, instead, I wonder: "What's going on in her life? How can I respond to her request for help?"

This is an effective result of his own self-awareness, his own Witnessing.

J: What I'm noticing is you were able to access empathy, even when you might previously have risked experiencing it as an attack.

G: In our new organization design and direction, I know I'm going to have challenges. I might have new role at some point. Right now I feel like it's easy. I'm in a flow state. These ideas, mindfulness, are coming more naturally and readily.

It was remarkable to be a witness to Gregor's review of his current situation and development. He was deepening awareness of the skills and approaches he was using. He realized how much he was benefiting by regarding this time of change with such equanimity. The future was still unknown, but he would be facing it from a position of self-acceptance and confidence.

Many busy leaders leave self-reflection to chance too often. Having an opportunity to notice one's inner calling, dilemma, satisfaction, or unmet need leads to a richer life. Some clients speak of "coming back home" to themselves. Others want to leave a legacy. Others find the deepest satisfaction in mentoring and developing staff; They realize that, though important, concrete results are less essential to self-esteem.

Strong leaders can be shocked when they receive a performance review that is less than stellar. Nathan had trouble considering the feedback because it seemed so unfair and so inconsistent with the rest of his professional career. He also felt betrayed by agreeing to a more junior title at the time of his offer with promises of future promotions that never came. To make matters worse, new management brought in their cronies. All of this highlighted what mattered deeply to him, and it informed priorities in his next job search.

Simon had caught himself in a dilemma. He wanted a particular new project, but was reluctant to lobby for it. Although he wanted the project to be approved, he was not sure he wanted to face the risks involved. In addition, although he wanted the project all to himself, he also wanted to work on it with others. Simon is not alone; we are all a little complicated and contradictory.

Ashley was disheartened that her agency was not living its mission. She knew what mattered to her and perceived a hypocritical inconsistency between the organization's mission and its actions. Reflecting on how deeply this affected her, she was able to transform her disappointment into a source of empathy.

Barbara expressed wanting more time to herself. As a leader with a long and successful track record, admitting this aloud was problematic for her, yet gave her relief and new workplace strategies.

Charlotte was destabilized by a lack of clarity in her role. It can be challenging to want to be helpful, yet also draw the line on scope of responsibility. She created clarity by envisioning a desirable future in which she is fully staffed and can return to a more strategic role. When things get hectic, it's easy for her to skip time to reflect. It doesn't feel immediately productive when those productivity alarm bells are sounding. However, when granted the time and opportunity to envision her desired future, her next steps easily came to mind.

Reflecting on his new pattern of communicating, Gregor was able to pull into focus how he was creating job satisfaction for himself. His new mindfulness and lack of defensiveness literally changed the dynamic of his challenging relationships. Needless to say, he was pleased with the result.

6

ZOOM LEADERSHIP AT THE MOVIES

In this chapter, we're going to have an opportunity to apply the Zoom technique by looking at movies through this lens of the four dimensions: Think, Act, Feel, Witness. By practicing the zooming as an observer, the technique becomes more readily available in your work. Note: The following passages include details of the films *The Martian*, *Saving Mr. Banks*, and *The King's Speech*—so bear that in mind if you have not seen them.

The Martian

The 2015 film *The Martian*, which stars Matt Damon as astronaut Mark Watney, opens with Mark and a crew of five others who live on a space ship/space station on Mars. When their ship is threatened by extreme winds, the captain decides they must evacuate. On the way to the ship, Mark goes missing. The crew determines that he must have been injured with a damaged space suit and could not possibly have survived the last few minutes exposed to Mars' atmosphere. Reluctantly, for the crew's safety, the captain decides to leave him behind.

Unbeknownst to the crew, Mark Watney has miraculously survived in spite of an antennae poking into his suit and abdomen. He staggers to the space station, where he can remove the suit and breathe normally. It is clear that his Feelings of being injured and scared are most prominent. He knows he has been abandoned for dead. He is panting and in pain. Yet somehow he has to override the Feeling modality with his Thinking; he must zoom from Feeling to Thinking to Acting. In order to survive, he must treat his wounded abdomen; in order to do so, he forces his Thinking to dominate his pain and fear. As we watch this self-surgery (or avert our eyes), we all know it takes superhuman effort to conduct this procedure without anesthesia.

Next, while recording himself speaking into a computer video diary, he declares he is not going to die—those are his Thoughts—and starts counting the food packets, so he can assess how long his rations will last (Act). He conveys his Feelings of optimism: "I'm lucky I'm a botanist. I have to grow three year's worth of food. Mars will come to fear my botany powers." Maybe he is Witnessing his own bravado or he's being motivated and reassured by it (Feeling). He was using humor to zoom out from his fear.

He moves into Thinking: "I need water, but I can make water because I know how." When his first experiment is a failure and blows up, he Feels stupid. Although he could become preoccupied with that Feeling and beat himself up, panic, or give up, instead Thinking takes over and he declares, "I'm going to have to science the shit out of this, that's my only option." That's a real zoom: changing a noun into a verb that emphasizes Action.

Later, following another disaster, he again Acts: he counts the remaining food rations, and counts them again. Acting provides reassurance about how much food remains.

As the film progresses, he Witnesses his "firsts": He zooms in to a sense of awe and wonder. "Everywhere I go I am the first. I am the first person to be alone on an entire planet." When he finds a way to communicate with NASA as well as his crew (still in their ship in space), he asks them to pass along a message: "Tell my parents when I die that I love what I do. It is bigger than me." This is Witness: the sense of purpose and belonging in the universe. The sense of awe. Even as he knows his survival is at risk, he can Witness what matters to him—and that he has played a part in such a vast endeavor.

NASA engineers on earth work with Mark to help create a rescue plan. In order for the old space ship still remaining on Mars to have enough lift to meet the rendezvous of his crew's space ship, the engineers create a model of what Mark needs to discard so the capsule isn't too heavy to takeoff. The instructions include removing the space ship's nose, the door, and most of the controls. Pretty much all that's left is his chair. "What are you crazy, you want me to rendezvous with my crew in a convertible?" The Feeling of fear drives his incredulity. Then he reflects on what they told him: He will become the first man to travel this fast in space. "I do like the way that sounds—I like it a lot." He shifts his attention from Thinking that it's lunacy to Feeling excited about making history.

Mark does survive and, in the closing scene, he is seen instructing a batch of new recruits on earth. He teaches them how to zoom into the present and take Action in the event of a disaster—which he assures them does occur. "You do the math," he declares. "Then you solve one problem then another."

Saving Mr. Banks

For twenty years, Walt Disney pursued the movie rights to the book *Mary Poppins*, by P. L. Travers. The 2014 Disney film *Saving Mr. Banks*, which starred Tom Hanks as Walt Disney and Emma Thompson as P. L. Travers, tells of the author's family background through flashbacks while detailing her resistance years later to the movie adaptation of her children's book.

Walt is determined to convince Travers to allow him to produce *Mary Poppins*. At first, his metaphorical camera is zoomed in on time and tenacity. Every year for twenty years he writes to her to ask to buy the movie rights. She declines. Then he zooms in on his own motivation: He had made a promise to his daughters twenty years earlier that he would make the movie. "Twenty long years, and that's what being a Daddy is, keeping a promise to your children. I have never gone back on a promise." He zooms in to his own Feeling of what it is to be a father—pride mixed with disappointment. Mrs. Travers remains unmoved.

Then he shares his delight, zooming in to the gift—the joyful feeling her book has given him: "When my girls were giggling their heads off I asked to read the book and my imagination caught fire. My imagination has burned ever since. It wouldn't just be for my girls, but for children everywhere, and adults too. Mary Poppins is going to fly off the page and you will hear her sing." Mrs. Travers objects, "I won't have you turn her into one of your silly cartoons." She has zoomed in to her own feeling of protectiveness and even gravitas for the role Mary Poppins plays. "Mary Poppins is the opposite of frivolous. She deals with honesty."

It is only when her own agent reminds Mrs. Travers of her financial status—she is out of money, royalty payments are no longer coming in, and keeping her home is at risk—that she considers responding to Walt Disney. The agent zooms in on Thinking "(You don't have enough money to keep this flat") and the Feeling of being obligated ("You have to go meet him—you have made a verbal commitment to sign the contract to the screen rights").

Once she arrives in Hollywood for two weeks of working with the screenwriters, Mrs. Travers (who repeatedly insists on this name, not Pamela), is difficult to please. Walt zooms in on trying to make her happy, despite her curt demands. (He reassures her they can change the view of the house, eliminate the color red, change the lyrics to the song, etc.) Since she has not yet officially signed over the rights, he must continue to convince her of the care with which he intends to treat her story. He zooms in to his own empathic Feeling of authorship—when his first Mickey Mouse character was purchased by a big production house. "I thought it would kill me to give him up." Still, she is not happy and returns to her home in London after only two weeks without having signed the contract. Walt says, "I am wondering what it will take to make you happy and you are probably wondering that too."

As Walt reviews her expense reports, he notes that her passport and ticket are not in the name of Mrs. Travers at all, but that of "Helen Goff." Zooming in to Thinking (finding the facts), he discovers that Helen Goff's father was named Travers, so she has taken his first name as her last name. (There is no explanation of how she becomes Pamela instead of Helen.)

Walt gets on the very next plane to London. He zooms in to her Feeling of attachment and devotion to her father (who was an alcoholic and died of tuberculosis when she was only seven years old). This gives him the opportunity to relay the story of his own challenging childhood, his father's harshness toward him. His Feelings about his own father opened empathy for her complicated Feelings about her father. Walt shares his insight with Mrs. Travers that in the story Mary Poppins has not come to save the children, but rather, the father—Mr. Banks. Now at last, having tried shining the light on his own agenda ("I made a promise"), the happiness she will give to others ("children and adults all around will love this"), and accommodating her screenplay demands ("all right, we won't include cartoons"), he finally discovers what may release her from resistance. He zooms in to acknowledge her mixed Feelings of sadness and devotion to her father. Walt promises to portray Mr. Banks with compassion and respect. "The last thing I would do is tarnish what I cherish. You have got to share Mary Poppins. Let's all go on and not have a life that is dictated by the past." It is zooming in to the real source of her reluctance that finally frees her enough to agree to the movie.

The King's Speech

Prince Albert might have been able to tolerate his debilitating speech impediment, a stammer, if not for two events in history. The first was the invention of the radio in 1925; it became the new vehicle for public speeches made by the Royal Family. The second event was that his older brother, who was in line for the crown, recused himself from the royal succession due to his scandalous relationship with an American divorcée. The 2010 film *The King's Speech*, which stars Colin Firth as Prince Albert and Geoffrey Rush as Lionel Logue, his speech therapist, tells the story of the would-be king's battle against his speech impediment.

Albert is desperate for help, but at first he is reluctant and resistant. His wife, Elizabeth, hears of Lionel Logue through the Speech Therapist association after all other attempts have failed.

Lionel is different from the start. Instead of treating Albert as his king, he insists on calling him by the family's nickname for him: Bertie. The king wildly objects, but Lionel is zooming in to Thinking about equality, rather than the more common focus on the gap of their status (Think). Lionel declines Albert's insistence that Lionel come to their royal home, instead saying they must come to his basement apartment for treatments. He is zooming in on having Albert regard him as the speech therapist authority (Think). He also insists that treatments occur on a daily basis because he Thinks that is what is required to be effective.

Meanwhile, Albert becomes angered by Lionel's lack of deference and his imposition of rules. For example, Lionel forbids smoking ("my castle my rules") and says, "I haven't agreed to take you on yet." Albert's sole expectation is vocal instruction, so he regards Lionel as intrusive when he asks about his first memories of when the stammering first occurred. Lionel has him read Shakespeare while wearing headphones playing a symphony (jamming Albert's ability to Think and stammer) and hands him the recording as Albert storms out of the door.

Later, following another frustrating speaking scene, Albert listens to the recording at home for the first time and is surprised at the sound of his own verbal fluency reading Shakespeare. This convinces him to return to work with Lionel. The treatment zooms into Action: Lionel works to improve Albert's fitness and muscle tone by rolling on the floor, swinging arms in time to music, shaking his jaw and head, and vocalizing vowels out the open window. All of this zooming in to Action is designed to disrupt the pattern of stammering while speaking (his old Action) which had been instilled from about age four.

Albert returns to Lionel when he becomes concerned about his brother's private life in the face of the impeding succession of King George V; their father is dying. Albert became frustrated that he didn't speak back after his brother insulted him. Now that Albert's deep-seated obedience to obligation and proper behavior is identified as a factor in Albert's speech impediment, Lionel zooms in to encouraging Albert to swear mightily. Zooming in to an unfamiliar and liberating Action helps him overcome this aspect of his speech challenge.

Once his older brother David renounces the throne, Albert reconnects with Lionel to prepare him for the coronation. One of Albert's advisors has investigated Lionel's background and tries to discredit him by saying he's not a real doctor. Lionel provokes Albert by flouncing into the royal throne. In essence, he zooms to Action in order to zoom Albert into Feeling. Albert rages at him, speaking angrily and flawlessly without hesitation or stammer. Albert has zoomed out of his normal pattern of proper behavior into a genuine Feeling: outrage. In doing so, his speech improved.

The movie ends with another zoom, in which Albert—now King George VI—thanks Lionel for being his friend. He is virtually his only true friend in a world surrounded by formality. Lionel acknowledges the new relationship by zooming away from the informality of the nickname Bertie and calling him "your majesty."

7

Applying the Model

Zoom Leadership is more of a guided intuitive process than a decision tree. Leaders may use it with themselves, as well as with their staff to help them expand their Thinking and bring a fresh perspective to a challenge. Leaders are also encouraged to use it with a peer learning partner, human resource professional, or coach. Zoom Leadership helps explore new perspectives and pays attention to *attention*. This might also extend to include where and how to "spend" attention. The careful spending of attention, or focus, is an important element in effectiveness (and joy).

Two common but stressful responses to the current conditions of information overload are being over-focused or, conversely, overwhelmed. To over-focus on something that is not critical in the long run (for example, someone canceling an appointment, or being late for a meeting) uses up valuable attention and energy. In those cases, using a long-term timeline can literally put things in perspective. However, not focusing—in other words, using too wide a lens to take in lots of information—can result in being overwhelmed, which can be paralyzing.

Even though it is not a step-by-step process, there are touch points in Zoom Leadership. The approach involves providing new options by identifying where the challenge resides.

As you consider the incident that is on your mind, reflect on the words and energy to identify which lens (or "lens point") to start with:

1. Think
2. Act
3. Feel
4. Witness

If it's not yet obvious which lens is the most compelling, Thinking is a good place to start because so many leaders and knowledge workers rely on their intellect.

Is there over-focus or a feeling of being overwhelmed?

1. Over-focus limits options and possibly important context. Therefore, zoom out and see how the wider landscape opens possibilities.
2. Overwhelmed results from taking in too much about the challenge. Therefore zoom in and consider fewer factors.

Can the light of attention be placed somewhere else?

3. If the light of attention is on others (the boss, for example), what happens if the focus shifts to self?
4. If the light of attention is on a co-worker, what happens if the focus is on clarity of expectations?
5. If the light of attention is the project, what happens if the focus shifts to the whole job?
6. If the light of attention is on the job, what happens if the focus shifts to the mission?
7. If the light of attention is on productivity, what happens if the focus is on play?

Very often a challenge may involve more than one of the lenses: Think, Act, Feel, Witness. The main benefit of zooming in or out—or shining the light on another element in the story—is that is unlocks what has become a limited view that may have been inhibiting options and creative problem-solving. In neurological research literature, this new view (or reframe) is referred to as *cognitive reappraisals*—the ability to generate options, even when emotionally challenged. In the research, participants are encouraged to write down as many options as possible when faced with a hypothetically aggravating situation. In business, leaders often don't have the luxury of time to consider a list of options, and don't need hypothetical challenges because there are plenty of real ones. A quick technique to introduce a new perspective can also result in considering multiple options.

It's nice to know that research about how the brain works supports the benefits of any kind of reappraisal or reframing which, in turn, enables the exploration of options. Some other studies focused on testing creativity by having participants list as many creative uses for ordinary items they could think of. As they did so, they were monitored on fMRI's (functional magnetic resonance imaging, which uses blood flow in the brain to measures brain activity) to determine which region of the brain was activated. This research is congruent with the concept that a change in focus activates the creative parts of the brain, resulting in new options, ideas, and possible solutions.

To make the zoom techniques easy to use, the new perspectives are presented here as separate views on the lens (elements of inquiry). After using the approach to open up new possibilities, it is important to consider the whole-person point of view. No one point of view will be comprehensive enough to empower leaders. Rather, using one lens at a time is designed to provide an easy-to-use way of generating alternative perspectives. The elements (lenses), of course, interact and do not exist separately from each other. Rather, this is a creativity tool designed to bring new focus when someone is stuck on a problem.

Leaders naturally reintegrate their ideas into the whole context once there is a new view of the issue. The altered focus can be incorporated into other tools the leader may already use, such as budgeting, project planning, strategic thinking, pricing or competitive analysis. It can also be combined with tools consultants and coaches may use, such as Myers-Briggs or the Thomas Kilmann Conflict Model.

Think and Feel

Think and Feel can be considered opposites on the lens views. They don't need to be, as Thinking and Feeling very often inform each other. If an issue seems to show up mostly in Thinking language, then exploring that same issue from Feeling can reveal new possibilities. For example, a leader named Charles reported this experience:

> C: (Charles): I've been kind of fried since the disaster this weekend. Some stuff I delegate and it's easy. I have check-points, milestones. I can tell what Joshua did. What a relief. When it comes to delegating other stuff, I'm on the fence about them. They're harder to pass down, emotionally. It gives me satisfaction to do them myself. I'm not sure I really want to get rid of it, even though I know Joshua can handle it.
>
> J (Janet): What are you thinking about that?
>
> C: Well, it feels more powerful—when I make the choice. I like doing it, it gives me a sense of satisfaction, but then when I think about the choice of being more strategic—using my "strategery"—it feels good.
>
> *I notice he is already moving between Thinking about options and Feeling fried, Feeling relief, and Feeling satisfaction. He is even aware of Feeling torn, as he analyzes his delegating options.*
>
> J: If you were to delegate, what would that enable you to think about and focus on?
>
> C: For one thing, I've changed the way I keep track of my to-do list. I realize I was serving it up to my inner bully—my inner critic. Every time I looked at that long list in front of me, it was like someone was criticizing me. Only it was *me*. So I decided to change that. I reviewed and reprioritized the list, and then put the

real ones—the ones I'm really going to work on this week—in front of me. The rest I saved and will re-evaluate at the end of the week.

Charles has noticed (Witnessed) that his Feeling anxious about his long to-do list comes from Thinking about how much he has not completed. Therefore he has Acted differently. He has simply changed how he keeps track of things and how much focus is being devoted to pending projects.

Act and Witness

Act and Witness can be considered opposites on the lens: Taking action is quite different from reflecting. Yet Witnessing can inform an Action, or bring new meaning to an Action.

Larry was a corporate lawyer for a pharmaceutical company. He was valued for his rigor and knowledge, but was receiving criticism for his communication style. Complaints included that he read and typed emails in meetings, and could lose track of deadlines and commitments.

J: (Janet): What would be helpful today?

L: (Larry): I find role-play useful. Reading. Internet research, even for things like communication skills. They work better for me than workshops.

Larry is already Witnessing his preference for Action.

J: What do you know about what you would like to be able to do differently?

L: I'm not always pleasant when I'm stressed, yet I don't mind the rush. I enjoy the nature of the work. There is enjoyment in finishing up something to meet the deadlines, but my stress level is not always managed.

He is Witnessing his Feelings of stress, as well as his enjoyment of the Actions.

J: What do you notice when stressed?

L: I can just feel it. Sometimes I react to pressure by trying to do it all myself, instead of delegating. Then I become "time poor." My manager and I have talked about that. For my career, it's critical to enhance my delegation skills. It's a challenge.

J: What have you already tried?

L: Trying to delegate when possible. It's difficult because sometimes it means giving work to more senior executives. Our distinguishing feature is that we staff thinly, but with senior people. So they are capable, but not always available. And I like the visibility if I can work with senior execs.

J: So you keep it?

L: Yes I tend to keep the work, when I know I should spread it around more. I have a tension with the balance. Wanting more help but taking on the projects I like.

J: When have you been able to notice that tendency?

L: I actually liked the Myers-Briggs (personality profile) we discussed last time. It's almost mathematical quantifiable. I notice how internally focused I am. I enjoy thinking by myself.

I am Witnessing that he integrated the model in a way that made sense for him. Did he Act on that awareness?

J: How have you used that to help with the challenge of delegating and communication?

L: I've realized I have to always be selling. Even though I'm in-house, I have to find out what people need, convince them I can do it, and then deliver. Extending myself in that way is a challenge; it feels exposed, kind of bragging.

J: What's an example?

L: The other day Harry came to our department. He was asking for one of the other lawyers, which kind of disappointed me. He said he wanted a lawyer who didn't do too much lawyering.

J: What do you think he meant by that?

L: I'm not sure – I know Harry is sociable, easy to talk to. I think he meant the connection was more important than the project. But I knew I could handle the matter.

Larry is Witnessing the Action that Harry prefers.

J: How do you want to respond to him?

L: I really don't see how the connection can be more important—unless he means making sure I understood his goals. I guess that could be it.

J: What would help him have that experience?

L: Maybe if I could let him get his whole story out before I start trying to solve the problem in my head. I start thinking about past cases and how I could approach things, but maybe I miss what's important. I could ask more about the outcome, what he wants to happen, rather than educate him about the law right away.

This Witnessing came with ideas for new Actions.

In this way, two of the four lenses combined to provide Larry with new approaches because he had a goal. He wanted to create a new reputation—being a more attentive listener—by suspending problem-solving until the connection was more firmly established. He had another challenge: delegating away projects that might be satisfying for him to work on. Witnessing his own reluctance—and the payoff—will allow him to experiment with ways of doing that.

Epilogue

We all know how to change perspectives; this is really the key to learning. Watch any toddler with a key and a door lock and you'll be able to observe Thinking, Acting, and Feeling. You may even Witness self-satisfaction.

This ability is innate, but may be overridden by habits of thinking. I offer a framework that has worked well with my clients, in the hopes that others will find that it provides easy access to new leadership approaches. How people feel about their work often stems from how they are treated by their managers. Managers have complex and unpredictable challenges to face. The more readily accessible leadership approaches they have, the greater the benefit to their staffs, supervisors, and companies—as well as themselves.

Learning is humbling; it requires being able to admit not knowing. In my role as coach, my clients are bright, skilled, and expert at what they do, and I'm offering them something new to consider. To remember the awkwardness of being a trainee while also being an expert, I try to learn something new and rather intimidating every year for myself. In the last few years I've tackled the following:

- Conversational French
- Roller blading
- Glass fusing jewelry
- Gospel singing
- Improv Comedy
- Encaustic art (with melted wax)
- Graphic facilitation (drawing what management teams discuss and decide)
- Book publishing

These were all things that were new to me when I first attempted them, which meant I had very little skill and they were challenging, to say the least. But they also reminded me about my motivation for learning, which made them fun. At the same time, these beginner activities also reminded me that learning something new can often result in these Feelings: clumsy, frustrated, uncoordinated, impatient, surprised, and delighted. Remembering these Feelings are normal for everyone—whether for business or at play—helps me be empathic when clients are learning new approaches to leadership problem-solving. I recommend that leaders try new fun activities as well. Not only will it serve the same purpose of viscerally remembering being in a trainee role, it also is a source of mental relaxation. Too many leaders don't provide themselves leisure time. It's an important source of renewal.

Deepening the Zoom Leadership Technique

As you work with the Zoom Leadership technique, the habit of altering focus and perspective will become more routine—not just in business, but also in your personal life and leisure activities. You may find that you apply it to a book plot, a sports game, or a political maneuver. The main benefit is that zooming in and out puts flexible Thinking front and center when you need it most. This ability will provide access to insights and collaboration that may not have been as available.

Leaders who work with this will find that their abilities to explore and discern will deepen. The approach can become more nuanced, combining two lenses—for example, Thinking and Acting, or Thinking and Feeling.

You may want to experiment with custom applications in functional areas, such as customer service or accounting. Strategic planning may benefit from looking at options through several lenses. Professional development conversations between manager and employee may become more relevant and meaningful, using this technique.

I would like to hear about what you discover. Please share your stories of how you have applied it Zoom Leadership. My website URLs, where you may find additional resources, are:

www.TranformationManagement.com

www.ZoomLeadership.net

janet@TransformationManagement.com

Sources

Chapter 1

1. *About the Hubble Space Telescope,* NASA. www.nasa.gov/mission_pages/hubble/story/index.html

2. David Rock and Dr. Al H. Ringleb. *Handbook of NeuroLeadership.* (CreateSpace, 2013).

3. Daniel Goleman, *Emotional Intelligence.* (New York: Bantam Books, 1995).

4. David Cooperrider, *Appreciative Inquiry: A Positive Revolution in Change.* (Oakland, CA: Berrett-Koehler Publishers, 2005).

5. Jerome Groopman, M.D. *How Doctors Think.* (Mariner Books, 2008).

6. Dr. Jacob Liberman, *Take Off Your Glasses and See.* (Harmony, 1995).

7. Alexandra Horowitz, *On Looking: Eleven Walks with Expert Eyes.* (New York: Scribner, 2013)

8. Stuart Brown, M.D. *Play: How it Shapes the Brain, Opens the Imagination, and Invigorates the Soul.* (New York: Avery, Penguin Group, 2009).

Chapter 2

Sureyya Yoruk and Mark A. Runco, *The Neuroscience of Divergent Thinking.* http://activitas.org/index.php/nervosa/article/viewFile/170/192

Chapter 4

1. Shawn Achor, *Happiness Advantage.* (Crown Business, 2010).

2. Carol Ginsey Goman *Think Leadership is Logical, Think Again.* Forbes 2014

www.forbes.com/sites/carolkinseygoman/2014/06/19/think-leadership-is-logical-think-again/#264329d17cc3

3. Chade-Meng Tan and Daniel Goleman. *Search Inside Yourself: The Unexpected Path to Achieving Success, Happiness (and World Peace)*, (HarperOne, 2014).

CHAPTER 5

1. Allison Gopnick, *Wall Street Journal*.

www.wsj.com/articles/when-awe-struck-we-feel-both-smaller-and-larger-1482418800

2. Williams, Florence. *To Fight the Winter Blues Try a Dose of Nature*, *Wall Street Journal*.

www.wsj.com/articles/to-fight-the-winter-blues-try-a-dose-of-nature-1485540954]

WORKSHOPS

Janet Britcher, MBA, President of Transformation Management LLC, offer a wide range of Leadership Development Workshops:

CHANGE MANAGEMENT

COMPASSIONATE COMMUNICATION

CONFLICT MANAGEMENT

DELEGATION

DIFFICULT CONVERSATIONS

EMPATHIC INTELLIGENCE

FEEDBACK

IMMUNITY TO CHANGE

INFLUENCE

MEETING MANAGEMENT

MYERS-BRIGGS

PERFORMANCE REVIEWS

RECRUITMENT

ZOOM LEADERSHIP

About the Author

Janet Britcher has extensive leadership, executive coaching, human resources and organizational consulting experience, and held leadership roles inside corporations for over 20 years prior to founding Transformation Management LLC in 2002. She particularly enjoys developing leaders being promoted, and companies which are growing.

Janet has an MBA with a concentration in organizational development, is certified in Myers-Briggs, Neurolinguistic Programming (NLP), LEGO Serious Play (a strategic facilitation process), Immunity to Change, Graphic Facilitation, and a Gestalt group process (The Cape Cod Model), Thomas-Kilman conflict model and 360 evaluations. Because she is a life-long learner as well as teacher, she continues to add to her tool kit of skills on leadership, communication, and management models enabling just the right approach for client challenges.

Janet is a devotee of Carl Jung's psychological concepts, and has been adjunct faculty in management at Lesley University and Regis College. She is a coach supervisor for William James College Executive Coaching program, a coach with the Executive Education program at MIT Sloan, and is a certified coach through the ICF. Janet brings an intuitive, spiritual and mission-driven passion to this work. She is a frequent public speaker.

Made in the USA
Lexington, KY
19 June 2017